D1617489

MERRY CHRISTMAS, PAUL
1981

LATER POEMS OF

Rabindranath Tagore

TRANSLATED
FROM THE BENGALI BY

Aurobindo Bose

———————————————

FOREWORD BY
YEHUDI MENUHIN

FUNK & WAGNALLS · NEW YORK

Printed in the United States of America
L.C. Card 75-34824
ISBN 0-308-10239-8
0-308-10245-2 (pbk.)

1 2 3 4 5 6 7 8 9 10

CONTENTS

HERMANN HESSE ON TAGORE

Tagore's partial eclipse in the West at the present time is a pheno-
menon based on a universal historical truth. Today's man of fame
falls into oblivion after his death, and only after a lapse of time –
sometimes prolonged – does the world take the trouble to re-examine
and reappraise both his former fame and his present neglect. Indeed,
the greater the fame the more obdurate the oblivion that follows.
This is the state of Tagore's reputation in the West today. In Europe,
in the years following the First World War, Tagore was not only
famous, he was also very much in fashion. But such is the world that
it likes to make its former favourites pay the price for gifts once
bestowed.

That is how the situation appears to me. In Tagore's case, however,
I see no cause for bitterness or complaint. He owes part of his
reputation to the rich heritage of ancient Indian philosophy, for
which he reclaimed a place of honour in the West, at least for a time.
In some minds and hearts the effects have lived on and borne fruit,
and this continuing influence – impersonal, silent and in no way
dependent on fame or fashion – may in the final analysis be more
appropriate to an Indian sage than fame or personality cults.

Although I had no close relationship with Tagore, I contemplate his
memory – that of a noble and venerable presence in the intellectual
world of his time – with affection and delight. And I would be happy
if I lived to see his triumphant re-emergence after the testing period
of temporary oblivion.

Montagnola
October 1957

FOREWORD BY YEHUDI MENUHIN

Above all what marks a great man is the spiritual climate he creates in his own soul; it is that repeated, almost uninterrupted, exercise which conditions his instincts and attitudes, his feelings, thoughts and actions, and finally his *aura,* that personal emanation which reaches out in ever-widening circles to inspire and to move his fellow men, even after his death.

The celestial orbits, the fiery sun, the gyrations of earth and moon are not more inexorable than the dedication of a great human being, man, woman and child, to his chosen way. For, indeed, as the compelling direction or purpose stretches into the future, so by the same token is it continuous with the past — an initial propulsion which already at birth gives the infant a life-direction.

The most revealing characteristic is the way in which the overriding compulsion, this self-made climate, sets its seal on the very smallest details of a life. In the animal world we do not wonder at that determined implacable thoroughness which makes an ant or a bird, an elephant or a snake, so uncompromisingly and so unceasingly ant-like and bird-like — in every manifestation of feature, organ or habit. Nor do we wonder at such obvious and visible conditioning by a lifetime's daily habits as the clerk's stoop, the monk's meditative gait, the farmer's patience, or the schoolmaster's compulsory restraint.

But we do stand in awe of the poet's and the composer's daily ritual. We revere that human being's personal church — the invisible, interior altar and chapel — wherein, in timeless order, first humility is practised and secondly inspiration is received.

Daily Rabindranath Tagore made room for the feelings and the thoughts of infinity — whether in love or prayer, daily he sought the reflection of the boundless and the sacred in the menial and the repetitive, transforming his measured words into a devotional exercise of symbolic grandeur.

Thus does inspired habit, practised over a period of time, purify and create; as does its antithesis — fire — consume and destroy. Truth is the quintessence of such contrasting phenomena as Shakespeare,

Bach, Beethoven and Michelangelo. These people speak the truth and we can trust them with all our hearts.

So it is with Rabindranath Tagore. As we read his poems we learn how infinitely good and comforting it is to trust in a human being. It is this very quality of trust in Truth, that is so terribly rare in the living person, which the young need and cry out for most.

As it happens, we may not only trust in the poems of Rabindranath Tagore, but fortunately for us, in the authenticity of their translations. Aurobindo Bose was a close friend and disciple of Rabindranath Tagore and is himself a person of integrity and distinction of mind and heart.

I am honoured to have been allowed to join this company and I pray that this book will gather into our ranks the anonymous reader, who will find the same inspiration, beauty and comfort that I have found in these verses.

London
January, 1974

Yehudi Menuhin

INTRODUCTION

The Life and Work of Rabindranath Tagore

I

Rabindranath Tagore was born in Calcutta on 6 May 1861, and died on 7 August 1941. His grandfather, Prince Dwarkanath Tagore, was a friend of the great Indian religious reformer, Raja Ramohan Roy, and one of the first Indians to travel to Europe, where he was received with honour at the Courts of both France and England. The poet's father, Devendranath Tagore, unlike the grandfather, was not a man of the world but a mystic and religious leader. The Tagore family have contributed greatly to the cultural life of Bengal, and the debt that Bengal owes to them is immeasurable. Poets, artists and musicians have come from this family, the greatest of them being Rabindranath, the youngest of a number of gifted brothers and sisters.

Beyond irregular attendance at two or three schools for very short periods — of which he had very unpleasant memories — young Rabindranath studied at home with private tutors. But he read much by himself when still a child, particularly the classics of medieval Bengali and Sanskrit literature. He could not, of course, understand everything, but the sounds of the words and the lilt of the metre, combined with his guessing of the meaning of Sanskrit words from his fairly thorough knowledge of Bengali, conjured up for him pictures of wonderful beauty. In later life, partly with the help of a German missionary lady but mainly by his own efforts, he managed to learn sufficient German to be able to read Heine's *Buch der Lieder* and Goethe's *Faust*. At the age of seventeen Tagore was sent to England, where he studied English literature under Prof. Henry Morley at University College, London. However, unlike many western-educated Indians of his generation, he did not write a line of English until he was fifty — and then almost by accident. After a severe illness, doctors had advised him to take a sea-trip, so in 1912 he sailed for England; during the voyage he made some translations from his poems for his

English friends. When he arrived in England, this brief selection came into the hands of the Irish poet W. B. Yeats, who was deeply moved by its beauty and depth of mystical feeling. In the autumn of 1912 the poems came out under the title of *Gitanjali* (Song Offerings), with an introduction by Yeats, and brought Tagore the Nobel Prize in the following year.

II

When Tagore was born, Bengal was astir with new life, which found expression in three great movements — religious, literary and national — all of which were later to be enriched by Tagore's own contributions. The religious movement was started by the 'great-hearted man of gigantic intelligence', as Tagore called him, Raja Ramohan Roy (1774–1833), the founder of the *Brahma Samaj* or 'Theistic Church of India'. Roy tried to reopen the channel of spiritual life which had become obstructed, fixed in external practices lacking spiritual significance. His was a strictly monotheistic religion based upon the teachings of the *Upanishads*.[1] He also believed in the harmony of religions and taught reverence for all the great religions of the world. In politics he was a true democrat and worked hard for the political and social advancement of India. Roy exerted the greatest influence in moulding Tagore's own ideals, and in innumerable addresses Tagore later expressed his deep indeptedness to him. Tagore's father, *Maharshi*[2] Devendranath, became the leader of the *Brahma Samaj* after Ramohan Roy died, and for this reason the Tagore family was completely ostracized by orthodox Hindus. This, the poet remarked, was a blessing for him, for it saved him from blindly imitating the past.

The second movement, a literary one, was heralded by the novelist Bankim Chandra Chatterjee (1838–84), who breathed new life into the moribund literature of Bengal, 'fettered by a rhetoric rigid as death'. Tagore says of him that

He lifted the dead weight of ponderous forms from our language and with a touch of his magic aroused our literature from her age-

---

[1] Sanskrit religious treatises dating from c. 1000 BC.
[2] His countrymen addressed him thus, which means 'the Sage'.

long sleep. What a vision of beauty she revealed to us when she awoke in the fullness of her strength and grace.

Thirdly, the National Movement expressed a spirit of revolt and of self-assertion against not only the political but the cultural dominance of the West. A generation of Indians, who had grown up under a system of alien education, had blindly rejected their Indian cultural inheritance. The National Movement aimed to rediscover the soul of India — it meant the revival of arts and crafts, the starting of new industries, the bringing of new life into decaying villages. Although it sought to rediscover India's cultural past, it was not a reactionary but a revolutionary movement.

All these three movements found active supporters in the Tagore family, among the poet's older brothers and cousins. In this challenging and invigorating environment the boy Rabindranath grew up, absorbing the music, drama and poetry that often filled the air of the great Tagore mansion, and here, while still in his teens, began his poetic apprenticeship. This atmosphere gave him above all the freedom to experiment, untramelled by hide-bound literary conventions. He also read extensively and wrote on the literature both of his own country and of Europe. From now on until almost the end of his life, a steady stream of poetry, drama, short stories, novels, literary criticism, social and political essays, religious and philosophical discourses poured from his pen.

III

In addition to his literary gifts Tagore was also an educationalist of the highest order, like Pestalozzi, and a born lover of children. He was a social reformer and practical idealist who had thought deeply on the problems of rural poverty and illiteracy, a patriot whose love extended beyond the confines of his own country and embraced the whole of humanity, a dreamer who cherished a vision, and a man of action who worked hard to bring the world a little nearer to the goal he had set his heart upon. In this many-sidedness Tagore can be compared to Goethe, a poet and minister of state who, among other activities, tried to ameliorate the conditions of the miners of his

Duchy. Both Goethe and Tagore loved and were deeply interested in Science,[1] hated narrow nationalism and thereby incurred their countrymen's hostility.

Bengali schooling at the turn of the century was a mechanical process: dry items of knowledge were hammered into the poor child's brain, and his vital needs – spiritual, artistic and practical – utterly neglected. Moreover, incredible as it may seem, most of the instruction was (in the towns at least) imparted in English. Tagore revolted against the entire framework and, in 1901, started his own school in the heart of the country, with five boys – two of them his sons. He wrote:

> We have come to this world to accept it, not merely to know it. We may become powerful by knowledge, but we attain fullness by sympathy. The highest education is that which does not merely give us information, but makes our life grow, in harmony with all existence.

In his school there was dance, song and drama, carpentry, weaving and gardening – activities all very revolutionary in the school curriculum of Bengal at the time. From America, he wrote to a teacher in 1921:

> I want just a small place where I shall try to build up a community of men and women who will recognize no geographical boundaries. They will know only one country and that country will comprise the entire human race.

In 'A Poet's School' he explained his aims further:

> I have tried to develop in the children of my school the freshness of their feeling for Nature, a sensitiveness of soul in their relationship with their human surroundings, with the help of literature, festive ceremonials and religious teaching.[2]

The essence of all true education is the relationship between master and pupil (*Guru* and *chela* in Indian idiom), and no curriculum of

---

[1] Tagore wrote the best popular book (in Bengali) on Nuclear Physics. His lifelong friend, the famous plant physiologist Sir J. C. Bose, FRS, ruefully exclaimed, 'Rabi, a great scientist has been lost in you.'
[2] 'A Poet's School,' in *Personality* (Macmillan, 1917).

studies, however perfect, can ever be a substitute for it. This was the ideal of the *Ashrams* of ancient India and also of Oxford and Cambridge with their Colleges and tutors. I, who had the unique privilege of being a pupil for five years at Tagore's school at its very beginning, want to testify to the ennobling influence of a great and loving teacher, whom we children loved and looked up to and did not fear. Today, Tagore's school has developed into the international university, *Vishva-Bharati*, whose motto in Sanskrit means: 'There where the whole world unites in a nest.'

In addition, Tagore started at Sriniketan, four miles away from the school, a centre for rural-reconstruction work. Tagore, at the turn of the century, was preaching unceasingly the message of self-help to his countrymen:

> Let us stop complaining about what an alien government has done or not done for us and cease sending begging petitions to it. Let us show to the world what we can do by our own efforts. For God only helps those who help themselves.

Nevertheless, he had to wait for almost two decades before a generous American, Mrs Dorothy Straight of Cornell University, and her future husband, the Englishman Leonard Elmhirst (a Cambridge MA and graduate in Agriculture from Cornell) were able to turn his dream into reality. Today, in independent India, the centre at Sriniketan has served as a model for the Indian Government's Community Development Projects and village rehabilitation work. Later, Dr and Mrs Elmhirst founded the famous Dartington Hall near Totnes in Devon. Elmhirst always said that his inspiration for this English foundation came from his previous intimate collaboration with Tagore at Santiniketan. During the horrors of World War II Tagore, just before his death, wrote to Elmhirst:

> History has awaited long for a perfect renewal of spirit, through the elimination of short-sighted nationalism. . . . I have come to that age when, in my dreams, I nourish my faith in the last survival value of friendship, of love. . . . Nations decay and die when they betray their trust — but long live Man.[1]

---

1 Some of the letters written by Tagore at this time are printed in L. K. Elmhirst, *Rabindranath Tagore — Pioneer in Education* (John Murray, 1961). They are a fascinating account of the friendship between Tagore and Elmhirst, revealing the scope and savour of Tagore's ideas on education.

Those who think that Tagore was always up in the clouds singing of love and the evanescent beauty of the changing seasons should have seen how practical and down-to-earth the poet could be, talking of the rotation of crops and village co-operatives with an agricultural expert from Cornell. And if further proof was needed to show his belief in the use of scientific methods to help the poor Indian farmers, it will be seen in the fact that he sent his own son, his son-in-law and the son of a very dear friend to Illinois University (1906-10) to study Agricultural Science. In those days, sons of well-to-do Indians were sent to Oxford and Cambridge to acquire English Culture, and the brightest sat for the Indian Civil Service Examination, then the entrée to the best paid Civil Service in the world. But Tagore had other ideas; his son was later to introduce tractors and teach scientific methods of farming to Indian peasants.

When Tagore was about forty, he became deeply involved in the National Movement and was successively President of the Bengal Provincial Conference (a branch of the Indian National Congress) and Chairman of the Reception Committee of the Calcutta session of the Indian National Congress. On many occasions he delivered important political addresses which aroused nation-wide discussion. He poured out in electrifying song after song the pent-up patriotism of his countrymen. But as the National Movement began to express itself through violence (at this period the Terrorist Movement first raised its head in Bengal), Tagore, disillusioned, suddenly retired from the political field. He was bitterly criticized for this action but he remained silent. I quote, in part, a letter he wrote to me in 1909 which throws light on his state of mind at the time:

I have the letter of ——— which you sent me. He is so annoyed with me that he has not even taken the trouble to read carefully what I have said. The supreme Truth and the supreme Good, that transcend all other values — I cannot sacrifice them to any temporary expediency, however high-sounding a name you may give it. Instead of establishing Dharma,[1] to place country above God and Dharma can never receive our assent following the example of Europe. . . . We must hold fast to the truth that country is not

---

[1] Religion, ethical conduct that guides one's life.

our God! . . . Patriotism can never give my *atma*[1] its ultimate sustenance. I have embraced Humanity, I can never let Patriotism gain the upper hand in my life. I proceeded a few steps along that path and found that I could not continue. . . . Don't feel hurt if people say hard things about me. God will make good all my losses. The more I lose, the more intensely shall I hold fast to Him.

IV

I now come to Tagore's poetry, about which I feel the least competent to write, having made my career in the field of Nuclear Physics rather than literature. It is only my great love for Tagore and his works that urges me to put down the few thoughts that follow.

There is no genre in literature that Tagore did not successfully attempt, but he will be remembered by posterity chiefly as a great poet and composer of songs. (Alas! these last can only be fully known and appreciated by the men and women of his *Sonarbangla*, golden Bengal, as he says in one of his songs.) His first book of lyrics was called *Evening Songs*. It contained all the vague sadness and pain of an adolescent soul struggling for expression. In reply to his critics he made these pertinent remarks:

> There is a period in man's life when his feelings have the pathos of the inexpressible, the anguish of vagueness. The poetry which attempts its expression cannot be called baseless. . . . There is a duality in man. . . . When the outward life fails to harmonize with the inner, the dweller within is hurt, and his pain manifests itself in the outer consciousness in a manner to which it is difficult to give a name, or even to describe, and of which the cry is more akin to an inarticulate wail than to words with more precise meaning. . . . These 'Evening Songs' are the history of that struggle. As in all creation, so in poetry, there is the opposition of forces. If the divergence is too wide, or the unison too close, there is, it seems to me, no room for poetry. Where the pain of discord strives to attain and express its resolution into harmony, there does poetry break forth into music, as breath through a flute. . . .[2]

---

[1] Soul
[2] Rabindranath Tagore, *Reminiscences* (Macmillan, 1917), p. 212.

Closely following *Evening Songs* came *Morning Songs*. The poems in this volume were the outcome of what one may call his first mystical experience. To quote his own words:

> When I was eighteen, a sudden spring breeze of religious experience for the first time came to my life and passed away, leaving in my memory a direct message of spiritual reality. One day while I stood watching at early dawn the sun sending out its rays from behind the trees, I suddenly felt as if some ancient mist had in a moment lifted from my sight and the morning light on the face of the world revealed an inner radiance. The invisible screen of the common-place was removed from all things and all men, and their ultimate significance was intensified in my mind. . . . The unmeaning fragments lost their individual isolation and my mind revelled in the unity of a vision. . . . I felt sure that some Being who comprehended me and my world was seeking his best expression in all my ex-periences, uniting them into an ever-widening individuality which is a spiritual work of art. To this Being I was responsible; for the creation in me is His as well as mine. It may be that it was the same creative Mind that is shaping the universe to its eternal idea, but in me as a person it had one of its special centres of a personal relationship growing into a deepening consciousness. . . .
>
> It gave me a great joy to feel in my life the mystery of a meeting of the two in a creative comradeship. I felt that I had found my religion at last, the religion of Man, in which the infinite became defined in humanity and came close to me so as to need my love and my co-operation.[1]

Tagore called this supreme Personality his *Jivan devata* – 'The Lord of his Life'. This conception of the *Jivan devata* plays a very important role in his poetry.

> Thou art the innermost spirit of my being,
> Art thou pleased, Lord of my Life?
> For I gave thee my cup
> filled with all the pain and delight
> that the crushed grapes of my heart had surrendered;
> I know not why thou chosest me for thy partner
> Lord of my Life!

[1] Rabindranath Tagore, *The Religion of Man* (Allen and Unwin, 1931), pp. 93, 96.

Didst thou store my days and nights,
my deeds and my dreams for the alchemy of thy art,
a string in the chain of thy music
(my songs of autumn and spring)
and gather the flowers from my mature moments
for thy crown?
I wonder if my failures and wrongs are forgiven.
For many were my days without service
and nights of forgetfulness;
futile were the flowers that faded in the shade not offered to thee.[1]

In India, through the centuries, side by side with the orthodox sects, there have always existed religious communities which did not recognize caste distinctions. They did not worship in temples nor make pilgrimages to holy places. The members of these unorthodox sects were often unlettered village rustics – both Muslim and Hindu. They had a simple and direct experience of God, whom they called *Nara-narayan*, 'God-man', and their songs have enriched the religious literature of India. Like the village singers of India, Tagore sought the Supreme Personality in his poetic creations, as well as in his practical activities. At first the idea of this Supreme Personality was vague and misty in his mind, but through religious experience it gradually took form and unified his life and his work. The history of this inner development he describes in his Hibbert Lectures, delivered at Oxford in 1930, under the title *The Religion of Man*.

The influence of the *Upanishads* on Tagore's spiritual development cannot be exaggerated. From the day the *Maharshi* taught (during their wanderings in the Himalayas) the boy Rabindranath to chant the holy verses of the *Upanishads*, the foundations of his religious education were firmly laid. Till his last days they were the inspiration and consolation of his life, and all his thoughts were coloured by them.

The *Rishis* (seers) of Ancient India knew that the human mind could never completely comprehend *Brahma*, the Absolute. There is one remarkably cryptic verse in the *Upanishads*: 'I do not think that I know Him, nor that I know Him not.' Another verse says:

That devotee conquers all fear who has experienced *Ananda*, the divine bliss of the *Brahma* — the *Brahma* whom no words can describe, from whom all words come back baffled.

---

[1] Translation by Tagore.

And although all words return baffled, unable to describe the *Brahma*, yet one *Rishi* breaks out in ecstatic joy:

> Listen to me, ye sons of the immortal spirits, ye who live in the heavenly abode — I have known the Supreme Person whose light shines forth from beyond the darkness.

Contemplating Him under the starry heaven of an Indian sky our *Rishis* realized Him as *Anandam* (Bliss), and sang:

> Who could have breathed or moved if the sky were not overflowing with joy, with love?

And they said:

> From God who is Bliss, are all beings born,
> Through God who is Bliss, do all living beings move,
> Unto God who is Bliss, do they (after death) proceed and enter.

Is not Beauty the supremest expression of *Anandam* — the idea taking form and illuminating the visible world? Have not all great poets strived after this Beauty, which is beyond mere sensual pleasure? We may recall Western thinkers who echo the same thoughts:

> A thing of beauty is a joy for ever. (Keats)

> Beauty is the shining of the Idea through Matter. (Hegel)

> The Beauty of finite things arises out of their participation in the eternal and ideal archetypes. (Plato)

A poet's *Weltanschauung* can never be confined within the limits of abstract philosophical categories — he scorns all 'isms'. For him holds good what Abt Vogler says:

> God has few of us whom he whispers in the ear,
> The rest may reason and welcome; we musicians know. (Browning)

W. B. Yeats has said: 'Whatever of philosophy has been made permanent is alone in poetry.' So we should not be surprised when Tagore confesses in his Hibbert Lectures: 'My religion is the religion of a poet. What I am going to say here comes out of an inner vision and not from knowledge.'

Tagore drank deep from the waters of this spiritual fountainhead. It was the vision of a *Brahma* who permeated with His immanent Presence both the starry heavens and the inner heart of man that gave wings to Tagore's poetry. Like those sages who composed hymns of praise to the sun, in whose effulgence they saw the glory of God, Tagore too could sing:

I know the joy that hidden in the heart of Light
Touches me, is one with my soul.
I have been annointed in the holy waters of Consciousness,
That flow from the font of Light,
And have my share of immortality.
In this multitudinous earth
I can be united with the supreme Me
And enter the path of Bliss.[1]

The *Gitanjali* (1913), which brought Tagore the Nobel Prize, is an eternal duet, between Thee and Me, God and the human soul. His religion is not one of quiet pietism or withdrawal from the world:

Deliverance is not for me in renunciation. I feel the embrace of freedom in a thousand bonds of delight.[2]

And he scorns the ascetic, who seeks his God in the flight from life. 'Who is there that thinks this secluded communion is the highest form of religion?' he asks:

Leave behind the chanting and singing and telling of beads. . . . He is there where the tiller is tilling the hard ground and where the pathmaker is breaking hard stones.[3]

In the *Upanishads*, *Brahma* himself is described as *Atmada*, the 'Giver of Himself' and as *Balada*, the 'Giver of Strength'. Therefore to him the poet addresses his prayers:

---

[1] *Wings of Death* (John Murray, 1960), p. 80.
[2] *Gitanjali* (Macmillan, 1913), 73.
[3] Ibid, 11.

O Giver of thyself! Give us strength to love fully our life, in its joys and sorrows, in its gains and losses, in its rise and fall. Let us bravely take and bravely give.

In *Sadhana*, lectures delivered at Harvard University (1913), he gives a poet's interpretation of the *Upanishadic* verses, important for anyone interested in Tagore's religious thought. He dedicated this volume to the Welsh poet Ernest Rhys (founder and first editor of the 'Everyman's Library'), who gives this testimony:

In Tagore you feel the humanity that was in the Son of Man, comforting the children of light in their awe of the Eternal. In him the spirits of the *Upanishads* reach the same threshold. It was natural that out of a living belief in the beauty of the earth, in sun and stars, and in the waters below, there should grow a living faith such as Rabindranath Tagore has expounded in *Sadhana*.[1]

And finally this last avowal of the poet:

To me religion is too concrete a thing, though I have no right to speak about it. But if ever I have somehow come to realize God, if the vision of God has ever been granted to me, I must have received the vision through this world, through man, through trees and birds and beasts, the dust and the soil.[2]

V

I shall now mention a few further volumes that are significant among Tagore's works. In search of the eternal feminine (*das ewig weibliche* of Goethe) Tagore composed *Urwashi*. The story is taken from Hindu mythology.

At the beginning of Creation
Out of the churning of the ocean,
Emerged two women —
The one *Urwashi*, the peerless Beauty,

---

[1] Ernest Rhys, *Rabindranath Tagore* (Macmillan, 1963).
[2] *Vishva-Bharati Quarterly* (August-October, 1949), p. 88.

The nymph of heaven,
Queen in the realms of Desire,
The other *Lakshmi* the Good,
The Mother of the world,
The Goddess enthroned in Heaven.

. . .

Urwashi, filling the cup
With the wine of fiery, boisterous spring,
Steals the hearts of men,
Breaking their meditation,
And scatters them wild
Among the blossoming flowers
And song of sleepless youth.[1]

The above is a short extract from the original, long poem, which is really untranslatable, so rich and flowery is the language. 'In her right hand she holds nectar, in her left poison. . . . She is neither mother, nor daughter, nor bride.' She is pure beauty, pure enchantment that draws the hearts of men, but she is always beyond their reach. The concept has some affinities with Shelley's 'Ode to Intellectual Beauty'. The late Edward Thompson (Lecturer in Bengali at Oxford, and Tagore's biographer) opines:

> *Urwashi* is perhaps the greatest lyric in all Bengali literature and probably the most unalloyed and perfect worship of Beauty which the world's literature contains.[2]

The two aspects of Womanhood – the Beautiful and the Good – have been pithily expressed in the extract quoted above. Tagore had a tender and idealistic attitude towards Love and Womanhood. In a late collection of love-poems, *Herald of Spring*, the fire of earthly passion, sublimated into spiritual love, has found intense and sustained expression. Love that gives strength rather than cloying sweetness speaks through these poems. And woman is not the frail creature, *Abala*, the plaything of man; she is *Sabala*, one full of strength and fortitude, who cries out: 'Oh make me fearless with the heroism of love.' And she is the comrade who affirms:

---

[1] *A Flight of Swans* (John Murray, 1955), 23.
[2] *Rabindranath Tagore — Poet and Dramatist* (O.U.P. 2nd ed. 1948).

23

> Your fetter I am not!
> I can give you company,
> For I am tireless and unwearied:
> I carry in my fearless heart the life-giving stream
> That can heal and minister.
> I am like the tree that draws water from the barren rock
> And pours it out in an unceasing stream of service.[1]

In their vigour, their undaunted courage and optimism, these poems remind one of Browning's *Men and Women*. The reader may also turn to numbers 7, 8, 9, 12, 14, 18, 25 of 'Poems of Wonder' in the present volume.

Soon after Tagore started his forest-school (*Ashram*) his wife died (1902). He bore this and many other bereavements with stoicism (next year he lost his second daughter and in the following years his youngest son and eldest daughter), and threw himself into the work of the school.

His deep grief at the death of his wife found expression in the short volume, *Smaran* (In Remembrance), written within two days of his bereavement; his love for his youngest and beloved son, Somi, in the volume *Crescent Moon*. These child poems are, I think, unique in the world's literature.

> When I bring you coloured toys, my child, I understand why there is such a play of colours on clouds, on water, and why flowers are painted in tints – when I give coloured toys to you, my child.[2]

His son, Rathi, has testified: 'Vicissitudes of life, pain or affliction never upset the equanimity of father's mind. His inward peace was not disturbed by any calamity, however painful. Some superhuman *Sakti* (spiritual energy) gave him the power . . . to rise above his misfortunes.'[3] Thus, when later I myself read Tagore's *Wings of Death*, written at his life's end, I could comprehend that what he wrote was not mere poetry; his life had borne eloquent testimony to his poetic philosophy.

---

[1] *The Herald of Spring* (John Murray, 1957), 86.
[2] *Crescent Moon* (Macmillan, 1913), p. 18.
[3] Rathindranath Tagore, *On the Edges of Time* (Longmans Green, 1958), p. 65.

When Tagore received the Nobel Prize in 1913 he was fifty-two. Soon afterwards, during World War I, a surge of new creative activity came to him and its first fruit was *Balaka* (*A Flight of Swans*). The essence of Balaka's message is that stagnation means death – life is movement, ceaseless change.

> As long as I am stagnant,
> I gather great wealth
> And never sleep,
> Like an insect I gnaw the earth,
> Heavier grows the weight of sorrow.
> Life, with its cautious brain and chill of doubt,
> Grows white with age. . . .
> Purified from that bath of Movement,
> I come,
> And drinking its ambrosia,
> Youth blooms constantly new.[1]

Bergson put forward this same philosophy of movement and change, but there is a fundamental difference between Bergson and Tagore. For Bergson, life is only movement, without a distant goal towards which it strives; it does not build a bridge from our finite self to the infinitude of God. But in Tagore, the human soul rushes towards its divine tryst:

> O homeless wanderer,
> The soundless melody resounds in your march.
> Do you hear the Infinite Beyond incessantly?
> Her love is terrible,
> Therefore you are homeless.[2]

Through countless failures, suffering and death, he approaches God, who is Bliss, who is shining on the other shore beyond death.

> The travail of the night,
> Will it not usher in the dawn?
> In the night of sorrow, under death's blow,
> When Man bursts his mortal bounds,

---

[1] *A Flight of Swans*, 18.
[2] Ibid, 8.

Will not God stand revealed
In his Glory?[1]

This short volume of forty-five poems is a landmark in Bengali litera-
ture, both because it introduces new verse forms, and because of the
wide sweep of its thought. We must always bear in mind the duality
in Tagore's nature – his longing for peace and quiet contemplation,
and the restless urge and will to action; the desire to realize God in
the beauty of nature, and at the same time to do battle against the
cruelty and injustice of Man towards Man. Out of this tension have
issued many of his finest verses.

His very last poems, dictated from his sick bed, were brought
together in *Wings of Death*. They reiterate one triumphant theme –
that in death there is nothing to fear. For the whole universe is Life,
shaped with a love over which death can have no power. The body's
death is but a new birth of the spirit into the great unknown.

VI

No one is more aware than myself of the inadequacy of my account
of the life and work of a man so many-sided as Tagore.[2] (At sixty
he took to the brush for the first time and painting became the
passion of his old age.) As a scientist, what I have most admired
in Tagore was his true understanding of Science, and his abhorence
of fanaticism in any form. He felt equally at home among thinkers
of the East and the West. Charity, humanity and clear rational think-
ing informed his conversation, sparkling with wit and humour. His
name *Rabi* means the sun, and he used to say that, like his namesake,
he rose in the East and travelled to the sunset shore of the West,
meaning that he belonged both to East and West. As he wrote, only
six months before his death:

> The wondrous sap of life
> Feeds the fields from many sources.
> Its dream and its awakening

---

[1] Ibid, 37.
[2] For further study, I strongly recommend Krishna Kripalini's biography,
Rabindranath Tagore (O.U.P., 1962).

Are circled by many streams of songs
That flow from East and West.[1]

Nobody worked more than Tagore for the resurgence of Bengali literature, and for the revival of the arts and crafts of our decaying villages. He sang of his motherland at a time when westernized Indians of his generation, blinded by Europe, slavishly aped the West. Yet the crowning glory of his life was the fact that he passed beyond nationalism and embraced the entire world as his home. On his seventieth birthday, in reply to a congratulatory address, he said:

I have not been born into a dead world. Mine eyes have never been tired of looking at the loveliness of this visible world, nor has there been an end to the supreme wonder! The eternal, deathless voice that has echoed through the ages — spreading over earth, sky, water — has found its full response in my heart. Leaving the narrow path of devotion to the goddess of Literature, I have gone out to serve the Supreme Man, the God-man, and brought him the worship of my works and the offering of my renunciation. I have come to the earth's great pilgrimage — here, at the heart of all countries, all races, all histories, dwells the God of Humanity.

A.B.

---

[1] *Poems of Wonder,* 39 (see p. 134).

TRANSLATOR'S NOTE

Most of the poems in this collection are taken from several volumes published during the 'thirties. Their division into 'Poems of Hope and Defiance' and 'Poems of Wonder' is my own – the former written at a time overcast with clouds on the political horizon and darkened by the triumph of dictators. These poems, I hope, dispel for ever the false idea that Tagore was a poet of the 'Ivory Tower'. They show the agony of soul he passed through during those years, reflecting 'what man has made of man'. At first, I thought of naming the selection 'Poems of Hope and Despair', but on closer reflection I chose the final title – for they breathe a note of defiance at the apparent victory of Evil over Good. The vision of

> Man Supreme,
> Man after God's Heart.

recurs again and again in Tagore's later works. In the poet's vision, the Creator had in his mind the 'Idea of Man' as he wished Man to be, not what he is in all his frailty. But though 'Man' has miserably failed, the great heroes and saints of history are there to remind him of his true destiny. This 'reminding us' is also the function of the poet, conscious of his God-given mission. Hence 'Defiance' and not 'Despair' reflects the true spirit of Tagore in these poems.

'Poems of Wonder' may again roughly be divided into two categories – one showing his deep and abiding love for Nature, infused with the immanence of God, and the other his chivalrous and idealistic attitude towards love and womanhood. The two final poems in this section are taken from *On My Birthday*, written and published in the year of Tagore's death.

Finally, I have included a selection of Tagore's songs – poems set to music by the poet himself. Tagore composed between 1,500 and 2,000 songs, and hoped to be remembered by them. To the Bengali race, he was the equivalent of Goethe and Schubert combined in one person – even the unlettered peasant sings his songs while working in the fields.

For each poem the name of the original volume and the page or poem number is given in the Sources section. A glossary of common Indian terms appears at the end of the volume. These words are italicized in the text.

It is my pleasant duty to thank the *Vishva-Bharati* for permission to translate the later poems of Tagore. All proceeds from the sale of this book go to *Vishva-Bharati*.

Ecole d'Humanité   A.B.
Goldern, Switzerland
August, 1973

To Yehudi Menuhin
Master of Tones

I dedicate these verses of a Poet
who was also a great Singer

Poems of Hope and Defiance

Incense yearns to disappear in scent,
Scent to cling to incense.
Melody seeks to fetter herself in rhythm,
While the rhythm flows back to melody.
Idea seeks its body in form,
Form its freedom in the idea.
The infinite seeks the touch of the finite,
The finite its release in the infinite.
What drama is this between creation and destruction —
This ceaseless to and fro between idea and form?
Bondage is striving after freedom,
And freedom seeking rest in bondage.*

---

* This poem served as an introduction to the first edition of the collected
works published in 1896.

1   *The Conqueror of Death*

From a distance I thought,
You are invincible and merciless –
The world trembling under your feet!
You are merciless!
Your devouring flame pierces the heart of the afflicted,
And your dart brings down the thunder.
With tremulous heart I approached you –
Your frown brought forebodings of approaching destruction
And the blow fell!
My whole being shuddered and I asked:
'Is there no more to come – your last thunder?'
The thunder crashed!
Is that all? Nothing more?
Gone was my fear.
When your sword was raised high,
I had thought you to be greater than myself –
With your blow you came down to earth
Where I stand.
Today you have become to me a petty being
And my fear is gone.
However great you may be
You are not greater than Death.
But I?
I am greater than Death –
Proclaiming this I will quit the earth.

O Lord,
Age after age,
Thou hast sent thy messengers to this pitiless world.
They proclaim:
'Remove all ill-will from your hearts,
Forgive and love.'
They are our masters,
And in reverence we cherish their memories.
Yet, on this evil day, I have turned them away
With an empty salutation.

I have seen:
Malice cunningly kill the helpless,
An insolent Might smother the voice of Justice,
Weeping in solitude!
I have seen:
Tender youth cry out in frenzied agony,
Dashing its head against the cold stone!

Today my voice is choked and mute is my flute –
My world has disappeared in an evil dream.
Therefore with tears I ask thee:
'Those who have poisoned thine air
And extinguished thy light,
Hast thou forgiven them?
Hast thou loved them?'

3   *The Call*

I ask again and again:
Where do you wait for me by the wayside?
Where in a solitary corner do you spread
Your mat for me?
Hearing your call in the air,
I have hurried to the dew-washed grass
Touched by the light,
And sought you amidst the rippling music
Of the restless river.
I have heard your flute again and again,
Where the clouds in many colours
Create their world of *Maya*,
Where shadows play in water,
And the dove coos on the *asath* branch.

As if searching me your trumpet called –
Yet my mind wakes not from her torpor,
Nor do I rush out to meet you,
But linger at my door in hesitation.

I have heard your call there
Where man stands humiliated,
Where the light dies in the heart of the afflicted,
And the prisoner cries in his dungeon;
Where the stone foundations totter,
Where buried fire shakes the earth
And the fetters of Ages lie shattered.

False Religion

Those who in the name of Faith embrace illusion,
Kill and are killed.
Even the atheist gets God's blessings —
Does not boast of his religion;
With reverence he lights the lamp of Reason
And pays his homage not to scriptures,
But to the good in man.

The bigot insults his own religion
When he slays a man of another faith.
Conduct he judges not in the light of Reason;
In the temple he raises the blood-stained banner
And worships the devil in the name of God.

All that is shameful and barbarous through the Ages,
Has found a shelter in their temples —
Those they turn into prisons;
O, I hear the trumpet call of Destruction!
Time comes with her great broom
Sweeping all refuse away.

That which should make man free,
They turn into fetters;
That which should unite,
They turn into a sword;
That which should bring love
From the fountain of the Eternal,
They turn into prison
And with its waves they flood the world.
They try to cross the river
In a bark riddled with holes;
And yet, in their anguish, whom do they blame?

O Lord, breaking false religion,
Save the blind!
Break! O break
The altar that is drowned in blood.
Let your thunder strike
Into the prison of false religion,
And bring to this unhappy land
The light of Knowledge.

O Traveller! You are alone –
How could you see the Unknown within you?
In the night you followed the path
Never trodden before;
You saw the sign in the sky
And alone you went;
You climbed the high peak,
From where the morning star
Sets forth on her voyage of light.

When in April heat the waterfall is born,
It has a vision of its far-distant future
Indescribable in beauty!
'I am! I am!' This refrain blossoms forth,
And hearing this call
The waters rush towards the Unknown.
Likewise, an unuttered message echoes within you,
And in every breath resounds the great yea:
'I am! I am!'

Great rocks bar the way,
Echoing the warning
'No! No! No!'
Waves thunder against lifeless matter,
Doubt raises its finger
And the coward shivers!
The sluggish mind conjures up fear,
And seeking safety rushes towards death.
In the narrow path of New Life,
You are the forerunner, ignoring all limits,
Conquering the impassable.
In every step resounds the great yea:
'I am! I am!'

With the hopeless cry
'Do not go!'
Whom do you call back?
Where is that bond
That can make the limitless, limited?
The world is like a flooded stream
That flows away, carrying everything
In laughter and tears.
'No! no! no!'
This cry is heard over the great sea of Time,
And resounds in the drum of *Rudra*, the Terrible!
O Mind,
Leave behind all desire, fear and grief –
The river of creation
Is but the endless flow of destruction.

Everything shall pass away –
Yet I love,
When in its joyous flow
The smile of existence gleams
In the midst of destruction.
From the *vina* of death
Pours forth the song of life,
Lovely in its restlessness.
From time to time, quivers the lamp of eternity
Illuminating the mirage of a moment.
The unplumbed river of tears bears on its current
The mother's love,
And the beloved's message;
In the battlefield of destruction,
The hero's courage is earth's treasure of beauty.
Time's duration measures not the worth of the gift,
Which the Infinite pours
Into the cupped hands of the transitory.

As long as it lasts
Value it with your whole life.
When the chariot of farewell sweeps past,
Forgetting self, make free the path,
Singing paeans of victory.
In the little earth you possess
Grieve not for what lies beyond –
It exists in the heart of the universe,
If not in one form, then in another;
Come out of your dark well –
Under heavens dome,
See destruction's blissful form.
O Sorrowful One,
The bubble of your grief shall float away
In the ocean of the Unsorrowing.

7 *The Free Path*

Move away, make free the path;
Your mind is heavy with the burden of doubt.
The stream of life flows lightly
With the music of murmuring waters,
With the frenzy of ecstatic joy.
Its waves alone lighten the burden of the Past,
And by their restless thrust
Straighten the tortuous ways of life.
Their clash
Sets free the tangles of life's net,
Cleanses all pollution,
And takes away life's weariness.

They are like clouds
Drinking in the morning light;
Like countless waves of the sea,
Like the exuberance of aimless winds,
Like the ceaseless flow of trees
That rejoice the heart of earth,
Like the first streaks of light
At the edge of ancient night.
They are children playing on the shore,
Maidens radiant in their youth,
Heroes who with courage conquer danger,
Their chains, echo the song of freedom
In their hearts.
They have no fears,
No worries for the future –
Over the future they are victorious.

At the call of the Unknown
From everywhere they emerge;
In darkness and in light
Rush to meet what lies ahead.
Begone, O Coward!
Bent under your burden of doubt.

Awake, O ancient East!
The moonless night of the Ages
Has mantled you in its deep gloom.
In your slumber you had vanished in the sea of oblivion.

Awake, O ancient East!
The many-toned melodies of life have ceased,
Like the dying notes of a cricket.
When shall the call of light
Dance again in your pulse?
Awake, O ancient East!

Who shall bring His message?
I am waiting for the moment
When the touchstone of the new dawn
Shall turn this earth to gold.
Awake, O ancient East!

With clasped hands I pray:
Breaking the shackles of old age,
May your new form bloom afresh
In the refulgent glory of the rising sun.
Awake, O ancient East!

The New Age is heralded with the call:
'Open, open the door! let darkness perish,
And lustre, born of sorrow and pain,
Shine forth in you.'
Awake, O ancient East!

9   *Lord Buddha's Birthday*

The world is frenzied with hatred
And torn with strife;
Its ways are crooked,
Of lust are its fetters.
O Great Soul, save them
Who long for thy re-birth.
Bring to them the deathless message,
And, nectar-filled,
Let the lotus of Love unfold its petals.
Serene, free,
Immeasurably holy and merciful,
Wipe away all stains from this earth.

Thou, the heroic Giver!
Come and initiate us
Into the path of austere renunciation.
Thou, the great *Bikhu*,
Accept as alms our pride.
Let the world forget its sorrows,
Tear away all illusions
And make luminous the sun of knowledge.
Let life return to the world
And sight to the blind.
Serene, free,
Immeasurably holy and merciful,
Wipe away all stains from this earth.

The heart of the whole universe
Burns in the fire of desire;
Naught can slake its thirst —
It withers away in worldly pursuit.
Stains of blood defile countries far and wide;

Hold over us your hand of blessing,
Blow your conch-shell,*
Play your benign melodies,
And bring the rhythm of Beauty.
Serene, free,
Immeasurably holy and merciful,
Wipe away all stains from this earth.

---

* In Hindu temples the conch-shell is blown to call people to worship.

The great machine made man a bird.
Earth, water are prostrate at his feet,
Only the air was left.

Wings are God's gift to birds –
Their joy blooms out in line and colour.
These travellers, many-coloured, are companions of the cloud;
They come of the same race as the blue sky's wind –
Their play blends with the wind's rhythm,
And their song with the sky's melody.
Therefore each morning,
Their waking mingles with the waking of life in the woodlands;
Waves to the rhythm of their wingèd dance
Play in the peace that floods the heavens.

To sky, forest, mountain –
From age to age they brought life's message.
But what has happened today?
Who knows its meaning?
Arrogance's flag, in pride of Power,
Has spread its wings.
The god of life has not blessed it,
The forest not made it her own,
And the moon respects it not.
Shattering the winds
And roaring in a shrill voice,
It announces its alienness to the sky.

Today, in Man's poisoned history,
It claims the clouds,
And in loud laughter
Rains from the skies destruction.
I feel the end of an Age has come –
Chaos, like the raging hawk,

Admits no impediment.
Jealously, cruelty, lighting the flames of death,
Raise terror in heaven.
If the place meant for the throne of God
Is desecrated,
Then O *Vajrapani,*
In destruction's furious flame,
Let the voice of the Terrible One
End Man's history.

O! Hear the pained Earth's prayer –
Let the song of the birds
In the blue-green forest ways
Once again tell its message!

11 *Penance*

Above ground – an electric, light-studded sky;
Underground (in the black and barbarous night below,
In that so-called civilized hell
Where plundered money is piled high)
The battle of the hungry against the full!
The earthquake's roar and unbearable heat
Shake the triumphal gate's foundation
And tear the treasure-house apart.
Swaying their extended hoods,
All the snakes from the underworld
Blow the fire with their poisonous breath.
Do not, vainly wailing, curse God;
Let first the furious All-Destroying*
Destroy accumulated sin.
In unbearable suffering
Let the bursting ulcer vomit its poison,
And vulture Science tear
At the bowels of the world.
One day those grasping, blood-red claws
Shall loosen their hold.
Cannibals catch at the crushed hearts
Which the weak have offered as sacrifice –
Torn, scattered bits redden the earth;
At the ending of that vast destruction
Heroic peace one day shall rise.
I shall have no idle fears
But shall calm the anguish that grew.
Through the allurements of pleasant ease
Weakness had gathered –
Let that be set on fire and turned to ashes.

The cowardly pious crowd the churches
To lull their God with flattery;
The weak-souled believe that by terrified prayers
They will bring peace into their homes.
The misers bring no offerings
But draw their purses tight;
They hope, by the magic of language,
To conquer the world,
And keep their gathered gains
By chanting holy hymns.
They hope to win forgiveness from God –
But He will not bear such insults,
Such false devotion.
If there is still might in the power of God,
Then, after penance in the sacrificial fire,
New life in a new land
Will bloom in new light.

---

* *Shiva*'s cosmic dance announces the destruction of this world steeped in sin, in order to recreate anew.

12　*Worship of the Buddha**

The drums of war resound.
The soldiers want to gather for *Jama*, the King of Death.
Their battle-dress terrifies,
They clench their teeth!
Restless with the heat of cruelty,
They seek His blessing
Who is the sea of Infinite Mercy.
Therefore, defiantly
They march to *Buddha*'s temple.
Trumpet and kettledrum pound with rage!
The earth trembles in fear!

Shouting, they pray:
May cries of anguish echo among the houses
Breaking human bonds!
May villages be charred to ashes,
And homes of learning ruined
By the sky's flaming rain!
For this, they proudly pray
To *Buddha*, the Merciful.
Trumpet and kettledrum pound with rage!
The earth trembles in fear!

To the rhythm of the victory-drum
The dead shall be counted;
Torn bodies of women and children
Shall rouse hilarious dancing,

---

* In a Japanese newspaper I read that the people were going to the temple
to pray to the *Buddha* for the success of their arms. They are aiming their
arrows of terror against the Chinese, and their arrows of worship to the
Buddha (Tagore's note).

And all breath be stopped by
The flying poison of the air.
With raised fists they march,
To make *Buddha* one of them.
Trumpet and kettledrum pound with rage!
The earth trembles in fear.

13

Earth, accept my salutation today –
My last, on the altar of ending day.
You are heroic, exulting in heroes;
You are lovely and severe,
Are man and woman mixed;
Shaking man's life with unbearable conflict –
With your right hand you fill the cup with nectar,
And with the left you shatter it to pieces.
Your playground rings with loud mockery;
The life of the hero, heir to a noble life,
You trouble and make hard.
The Good you make too costly to obtain,
And for the pitiable you have no pity.
The constant struggle
That you have hidden in your trees,
Displays its victory in fruits and grain.
Your merciless battlefield is on water and on earth;
There, in the face of death,
The victorious message of the conqueror is proclaimed.
Civilization's victory tower raises itself
On foundations laid by cruelty –
Its smallest fault is rewarded with destruction.
On history's first page
Unlimited was the might of the giant –

Of the man, the barbarian, the fool.
His fingers were coarse, his hands clumsy;
With club in hand he created utter ruin
On land and sea;
With fire and vapour he whirled evil dreams
Into the sky.
In the world of the inanimate, he reigned supreme –
Toward living things he was blind with jealousy.

In the next era the god arrived
And chanted *mantras* to tame the monster;
The pride of the inanimate was humbled;
Spreading her green carpet,
The goddess of life sat down.
Dawn showed on the peaks of the eastern hills,
Dark came down on the shores of the western sea,
Bearing the chalice of Peace.
Though the giant, chained, grew quiet,
That first barbarian lingers in your history.
In the midst of order he brings disorder,
Moving out of his dark cave;
His madness lingers in your pulse.
The *mantra* of the god resounds day and night
In deep, grave tones –
In sky, air and forest.
Yet again and again your serpent-demon,
Half-tamed, rises from your underworld
With extended, hissing hood.
Urged on by him you kill your own brood,
Desolate your own creation.
Both good and evil are established beneath your footstool;
Today I shall salute you – your beautiful, fierce glory –
With my bruised, humiliated heart.
With my entire body and mind
I touch, I realize
The hidden movement of all-embracing life,

All-embracing death.
Under that earth, through countless ages,
Have gathered the vanished bodies
Of innumerable men.
In that silent heap of dust,
That devours names and form,
And all that was once familiar,
I too shall leave behind a handful of dust,
The end of all my joys and sorrows.

Firm-bound world,
Sky-reaching world,
Meditating world
Sunk in the great silence of mountain summits,
Sea-girt world
Resounding to the unwearied, solemn music of the waves –
You are lovely in your abundance,
In penury terrible!
On the one side,
Your rice fields bowed with weight of unripe corn –
Its dew removed by the early gracious sun;
And the setting sun, leaving amidst the waves of grain
Its unspoken message: 'I am blessed'.
On the other,
The devilish dance of Illusion
Among skeletons, scattered in deserts –
Parched and fruitless, terror-pale!
In April I have seen your thunderstorm
Sweep like an eagle down,
To snatch horizons all away;
The sky like a lion roared,
At the beating of whose tail
The forest lay upturned on the ground.
Like an unchained prisoner,
The roofs of straw rushed off before the wind.
Again in Spring,

I have seen your cool, southern wind spread out
Among the scented mango-buds,
The song of meeting and parting.
In defiance of the storm,
The rustle of impatient leaves
Breaks out into a shout of joy.

You are loving and cruel, old and ever new.
From Creation's first sacrificial fire*
You rose up in an immemorial dawn.
On your pilgrimage, along your path
You have scattered many remnants of history
Grown void of sense;
You have spread out,
In layer after layer of oblivion,
Your discarded creations.
Protector of life,
You have nourished us in little cages of fleeting Time —
Within these are the limits
Of all life's play, all deeds' end!
Nor shall I claim immortality
For the garland I have woven day and night.
During the earth's journey round the sun
Countless moments come and go;
If to a moment of that great Time
I have given some significance,
If with extreme anguish I have conquered
Some fruitful part of life,
Then set a *tilak* of earth upon my brow —
That mark shall vanish on that night
When all marks vanish in the depths of the Unknown.

---

* The *Vedas* say that out of '*Jagya*' (fire-sacrifice) *Brahma* created the
world.

O indifferent, stoic World!
Before you forget me totally,
I touch your cruel, pitiless feet
With my last salutation!

16 October 1935

14

They have no caste,*
May not chant the holy verses.
At the temple's door,
The priests who ply faith,
Bar the way.
They search for God in his own place,
Beyond all barriers —
In the star-filled sky,
Flower-filled forest,
In the impenetrable sadness
Where lovers meet and part.
That walled-in, locked-in vision of God
Is beyond their reach.
In early life,
How often have I seen such a worshipper
On the banks of the Padma —
The river that restlessly corrodes
The old temple's strong foundations;
Seen him, *ektara* in hand,
Wander the deep and lonely path,
Seeking the way to the 'Man of my Heart'.†

A poet, I am one of them —
I have no caste,
May not chant the holy verses.
My worship never reached the prison-house of God.
The priest came to the temple and, smiling, asked:
'Have you paid respect to your God?'
'No,' I said.

---

* Hindu Society is divided into three castes; then come the Untouchables,
the casteless ones, who may not enter the temples, nor take meals with
those of high caste. Today this prohibition has been removed by law.
† The religious sect of the *Bauls* call God 'The Man of my Heart'.

'You do not know the way?'
'No,' I said.
'You then have no caste?'

I think to myself today:
Who is my God?
Whom have I worshipped?
I thought I had worshipped that God,
Whose name I had always heard,
Of whom I have read
In many scriptures, many tongues.
To prove my devotion
I have diligently worshipped Him.
Today I see
I have not proved Him in my life.
I have no caste,
May not chant the holy verses.
Reaching the locked temple-doors,
My worship wandered far away,
Beyond all barriers –
To the star-filled sky,
Flower-filled forest,
To the painful, rugged track
Where lovers meet and part.

As a child,
I received my first *mantra* of the earth's day of birth
(In the strong joy of my heart) –
The *mantra* of Light;
Received, sitting in my garden,
Alone in the ruin and mouldering walls
Amidst the swing of frilled coconut leaves.
Energy has fallen in waves
From the fire-fountain of primeval life,
And given me the shock of the Unutterable.
The dim message of immemorial Time

Has shaken my whole mind.
The bright rays of my unblossomed being
Have vanished in the vaporous body of the ancient Sun.*
Looking at the grainless, winter plains,
I hear in my blood's unrest
The foot-step of silent light.
That sound has followed me from my birth,
From the starting of most ancient Time.
My mind spreads over infinite Time in wonder
When I consider:
In Creation's pilgrimage of life,
I lay awake in that light,
Within which, innumerable Ages past,
My dormant future lay.
My worship has been fulfilled
Each day, in the joy of this awakening.
I have no caste,
May not chant the holy verses.

I do not know
To what my self-forgetful worship,
That lay beyond all ritual and creed,
Was dedicated.

Friendless as a child
And looking far away,
I lived my days in solitude.
I was born in a world
Unloved, unclean —
A world without walls and blazons.
My neighbours' homes were circled by high fences.
I was a nameless boy, an outcast,
They had fine and crowded homes —
From afar, I watched their coming and their going

---

* These lines recall the invocation to the Sun in the *Vedas*.

Along the paved way.
I have no caste,
And may not dine with them.
The men brought up in ritual and creed
Did not recognize Man in me,
Therefore I played on the streets alone.
Holding up their robes, they passed by,
And plucked flowers for the worship of their God –
Flowers plucked by the rules of their holy books;
And for my God, left behind
Flowers from all lands –
Flowers blessed by the same sun.
Neglected by the crowd
I have roved, hungry for unity with Man,
Whose guest-house has no walls, no guards.
Beyond the crowd I have found friends in my solitude –
Friends who in history's great Ages
Have come with lights,
Come with the Great Message.
They are heroes, death-conquerors,
They are my kith and kin,
My caste and my lineage.
By their constant purity, I am made pure.
They are Truth's pilgrims,
Light's worshippers –
Worthy possessors of *Amrita*.
In the narrow circle, I have lost Man
And found him there, where he transcends
The limits of all lands.
With folded hands, I have prayed to Him:
'O Eternal Man, you who belong to all men,
Save me from the arrogance of Pride,
That wears the mark of Exclusion.'

O Great Being,
I have seen you beyond Darkness

And am blessed.*
I have no caste,
No caste at all.

One day in spring, a woman came
In my lonely woods,
In the lovely form of the Beloved.
Came, to give to my songs, melodies,
To give to my dreams, sweetness.
Suddenly a wild wave
Broke over my heart's shores
And drowned all language.
To my lips no name came,
She stood beneath the tree, turned,
Glanced at my face, made sad with pain,
And with quick steps, came and sat by me.
Taking my hands in hers she said:
'You do not know me, nor I you –
I wonder how this could be?'
I said:
'We two shall build, a bridge for ever
Between two beings, each to the other unknown,
This eager wonder is at the heart of things.'

I have loved her.
One stream of that love
Has circled her in a cool embrace
Like the known, shallow village river.
That slow-moving stream
Flows beside low banks of the beloved's
Trivial and daily life.
Drought has often made it feeble,
Bounty of July rain has often made it full and loud.

_____

* A prayer from the *Upanishads*.

Dim with the veil of insignificance,
The homely face of the woman –
Sometimes I have loved,
Sometimes mocked and hurt.

The other stream of that love carries
The great Ocean's call.
Noble and generous woman emerges,
After a cleansing wash in those great waters,
From its depth.
In the form of boundless *Dhyana**
She has entered my mind and body,
Perfecting both my song and me.
She has kept alive eternal Separation's flame
In the hidden depths of my mind.
In its light I have seen her ageless grace –
Seen her in spring flood and flowers and leaves.
In sparks of sunlight
Scattered by shaken *sishu* leaves,
I have heard the melody
Swiftly struck from the *sitar*'s string;
On the changing season's stage,
In light and shadow,
I have seen her dance of many-coloured veils.

I have seen her seated near Creation's throne,
Seated to the left of God;
Have seen – when Beauty was insulted
By the unclean touch of the ugly, the pitiless –
The destroying fires shooting from *Rudrani*'s eye,
That scorched the secret nest of pestilence.

---

* These lines may be paraphrased thus:
To my inner eye she appears as the great ascetic,
lost in meditation – the inspirer of my Muse.

63

Day after day,
There has gathered within my songs
Creation's first mystery – Light's unfolding,
And Creation's last mystery – deathless loveliness of Love.

I have no caste,
May not chant the holy verses.
Beyond all temples' barriers
My worship is fulfilled today –
Coming from the realm of God,
Ending in the realm of Man;
Completed in the heavens in the Illumined Being,†
Completed in the closest joy in the heart of Man.

.

---

† One of the epithets used by the Vedic *Rishis* (Sages) in their invocation to God.

15 *Africa*

In that bewildered Age
When the Creator, unsatisfied with his creation,
Destroyed it time and again,
The wrathful sea separated you, O Africa,
From the bosom of ancient earth,
And He girded you with dense forests
Impenetrable to light.
There, in your inmost recess,
You gathered the mysteries of the Incomprehensible,
And unravelled the riddle of
Earth, sky and water.
The magic of Nature, beyond the ken of human eye,
Was maturing its message beneath your consciousness.
O sun-shaded Africa!
Shrouded in a veil,
Under the turbid glance of contempt
Your humanity lay hidden.
On they came with shackles of iron,
These man-hunters —
Their claws sharper than tiger's,
Their minds dark with pride —
Darker than your sunless forest!
The cruel greed of the Civilized
Laid bare its shameless humanity;
The tracks of the forest,
Ringing with your wordless cry,
Became soiled with blood and tears.
The nailed boots of the plunderers
Left behind their indelible mark
On your dishonoured history.
At that very hour, beyond the seas,
The church bells rang calling men to prayer;
Children played on mothers' laps,
And in the poet's song

Rang the invocations to the Beautiful.
Today, when the night is choked with thunder,
And beasts emerge from hidden caves
Presaging the end of an Era,
Come, O Poet of a New Age –
Stand in the fading light of the dusk
Amongst the dishonoured,
And proclaim: 'Forgive, O forgive!'
May this be your last message,
O Africa!

Amrita

At the time of parting I said to her:
'Once a woman of India* said:
She didn't want material possession,
She wanted *Amrita*.
This indeed was her vow!
What have you to say to that?'
Amiya smiled sadly and asked:
'What advice is this?'
Pressing her hands, I replied:
'Love is that *Amrita*,
All else meant nothing to her,
One day you will understand.'

Vexed, Amiya retorted:
'Why did you not take me away from Unreality?†
Why have you not the strength for it?'
I replied: 'It hurts my pride,
So long as I am not equal to you in riches,
I will not see you.'
Amiya stood up with a shake of her head
And left the room.
I said: 'Please keep this in mind:

---

* *Maitreyi*, wife of the sage *Yagyavalka*.
† This story is told in the *Upanishads*:
When the sage *Yagyavalka*, was (as was the custom in Vedic India) retiring
from the world, he wanted to leave behind for his wife material goods.
But Maitreyi protested: what would she do with all these material
possessions, when it wouldn't gain for her the soul's immortality; and
from her anguished heart issued forth the prayer:

From the Unreal lead me to the Real,
From Darkness lead me unto Light,
From Death lead me unto life immortal.

In this poem the suitor unscrupulously distorts the whole meaning of this
famous invocation to suit his purpose – he is a crass materialist!

As exchange for your love
I will not give you the dishonour of poverty,
This is my vow as a man.'

Day and night passed by,
The intoxication of the gold rose to my head.
The more I amassed,
The more I was thrust onward.
I could not stop or halt the force that drove me.
Wealth and fame both increased,
And with expanded chest I gave myself to boasting.
At last the doctor warned me:
'You need a rest;
The machine of your body is almost running down.'

I went to a far, lovely country.
There an arm of the sea
Ran up into the hilly forest.
The birds had crowded on the tree-tops,
Near the fishing place.
A feeble stream leapt from rock to rock,
And the rippling music of its waters
Made one grand tone of solitude.
The air, washed clean for ever,
Wandered from woodland to woodland
Humming a melody.
The coconut trees had formed a cluster –
Some erect, some leaning,
With fringes swinging restless,
Day and night.
The wilful waves foamed and dashed
Against the heavy, black rocks,
Scattering shells along the beach.
The fever of the body had left,
And the mind grew calm.
All the labour of the past seemed a fraud,

And life stretched out both hands
For the true gold of life.

That day the sea was calm –
The sun of autumn quivered
On the shivering blue of the sea.
Near my hut, the wind rushed wildly
Through the tamarisk,
And its leaves shook.
A mauve bird, with a dash of white on its breast,
Sitting on a telegraph wire and flicking its tail,
Sang sweet and gentle tunes.
In the clear blue of the autumn sky
Was spread the infinite sadness
Of some ancient exile.
Within me a voice called:
'I must return.'
And from time to time came back to my mind
The light that sparkled once
Upon her tear-wet eyes.

That day I took the ship.
Landing, I went straight to her home.
It seemed unoccupied;
I came to the main door
And found it locked;
My heart thumped.
From the house came the sigh of empty spaces,
And touched my heart.
After much search I found her –
A destitute village on the edge of an old pond
With a ruined temple,
Dim letters on its walls –
No longer witness to its past glory.
An ancient *aswath* embraces it in its tight grasp.

On the bank, under the shade of a banyan,
A new thatched cottage houses a girls' school.

I saw Amiya –
An ash-coloured, rough *sari* about her body,
Bangles on her wrist,
Feet without shoes,
Her hair hanging loosely down her back.
A rustic tan touched her face –
She was watering her kitchen garden.
I could find no words to utter –
Nor from her lips came greeting
Or any question.
Casting a sly glance at my costly shoes
She said simply:
'The weeds have covered the tomato shoots,
Stay away for fear you trample.'
I could not quite understand –
Was it in earnest or in jest?
On my wrists were pearl cuff-links,
I turned up my sleeves to hide them.
In my pocket I carried a brooch for Amiya –
It was clear – only a smile of ridicule
Would greet its diamond,
If I approached her to give it.
With a forced laugh I asked her:
'Where do you live?'
Putting down her water-can, she said:
'Would you care to see it?'
She took me through the school-building
To her room on the eastern side,
Separated only by a curtain.
On her hard, wooden bed
The bedding lay rolled.

On the stool was a sewing machine,
A *sitar* cased in chintz
Rested against the wall;
A mat was spread at the southern entrance,
On it lay scattered
Old bits of cloth, ribbons of many colours,
Mirror, comb and a flask of oil,
A cane-bag with odds and ends.
Against the wall in the southern corner
Stood a small writing desk,
And in a coloured earthen vase
A lotus.
Amiya said: 'This is my home,
Wait a moment, I shall soon return.'
Outside on the branch of the banyan
A cuckoo sang.
Behind the arum bush
Was a crowd of excited sparrows;
In the distance lay a pond
Glistening in the sun.
On the table I saw a picture
(A youth I did not know),
Drawn in charcoal, framed in glass –
Broad forehead, ruffled hair,
In his eyes the light of a distant future,
His lips tight with resolve.

Amiya entered with a plate –
Puffed rice, coconut cakes,
Milk in a black marble cup,
And juice from a green coconut.
She set the plate on the table
And spread on the floor a mat of woven wool.
I would not have been a lie
To say 'I am not hungry;'
It would have been the truth to say:

'I have no appetite,'
But nevertheless I had to eat.

Then I heard the story.

While my own money grew in the bank,
And I kept no account of my gaining and spending,
Amiya's father, Kunja Kishore,
Had from time to time invited to the tea-table
Sons of millionaires.
His self-willed daughter had frustrated again and again
Many favourable chances.
When striking his forehead
Kunja Kishore had thrown up his hand in despair,
Suddenly, on the family horizon
A homeless, mad comet appeared –
Mohibhushan, the only child of the *Raibahadur* of Madhpara.
The *Raibahadur* was famous all over the country
For his hoarded wealth and hardened heart.

No father of a girl could ignore his son,
However wild he might be.
After spending eight years in Europe,
Mohibhushan had returned home.
His father said: 'I am now old,
Look after the family estate.'
The son replied: 'What's the use?'
The people said:
'The Russian bat that chases away *Lakshmi*
Has picked the unripe fruit of his brain.'
Amiya's father said: 'No fear of that,
The moist air of the country is already softening him.'
Within a short time Amiya became his disciple.
Mohibhushan came and went when he liked –
Neither titters nor gossip affected him at all.

Day followed day.
Losing patience Amiya's father raised the question of marriage.
Mohi replied: 'What's the use?'
Her father said angrily:
'Then why do you come every day?'
Mohibhushan said simply:
'I want to take Amiya to her field of work.'

Amiya's last words were:
'I have come to his work.
He has freed me from the dungeon of material possessions.'
I asked: 'Where is he?'
Amiya replied: 'In jail.'

3 July 1936

Out of the dim past they have come in crowds —
Seekers and devotees;
Have come through the lion-gate of Time's long past —
Travellers and warriors,
Whose eternal journey is towards the future.
The battle has not ended,
The trumpet of Eternity resounds;
With the marching-steps of many Ages
The earth shakes.
At the dead of night the heart beats,
The mind grows listless,
Riches, honour, turn to dust
And death seems dear.
Those who had vigour in the marrow of their bones,
Those who marched on the great road,
Having crossed over death, still march today.
Those who clung to material things
Are the dead-in-life —
Their lifeless home is on the dumb sea's shores.

Who knows at what primary time Man came
And stood at the crossroads of the universe?
His sustenance was in his blood,
In his dreams,
And in the very path he trod.
No sooner had he drawn a plan,
And built on solid ground his home,
And raised, to touch the clouds, his roof,
Than the floor gave way, riddled with holes.
The dam that he built
The flood washed away;
The gains he counted in the night
Were losses by break of day;
The goods that he gathered to enjoy,

Caught fire and burned to ashes.
His ritual and his morals,
His chains and his cage,
Have been buried
Under the earth of past Ages.
Sometimes in the darkness
He has slept, half-drunk, in the couch of luxury.
Out of the dark, the evil dreams came down on him,
Throttling his throat like furious beasts.
In the pain of death he woke,
Smashed his wine glass on the ground,
And tore his garland into shreds!
Time and again, along the path
Impassable and slippery with blood,
Through the gaping centuries he strode out
Into the Unknown, into the Unseen.
In his blood the trumpet sounded:
'Beyond all borders, go beyond!'

Rod of Justice

Thy rod of Justice thou hast put into each of our hands,
And given us the right to chastise, O Lord!
This great honour, this arduous task,
May I humbly, with bowed head
Accept from thee!
In performance of thy task may I fear none.
Where to forgive is craven weakness,
May I be hard, O Terrible One, at thy behest,
And Truth flash from my tongue like a glistening sword!
Sitting on thy throne of Judgement,
May I keep unsullied thy honour.
He who does wrong,
And he who meekly suffers wrong —
May thy contempt scorch them both like dry grass.

A Sheaf of Songs

1

The cry that is in my heart is also the cry of her heart;
The thread with which she binds me binds her too.
Her have I sought everywhere,
Her have I worshipped within me,
Hidden in that worship she has sought me too.
Crossing the wide oceans she came to steal my heart.
She forgot to return, having lost her own.
Her own charms play traitor to her,
She spreads her net, knowing not
Whether she will catch or be caught.

2

Oh thou last star of early dawn,
Leave behind thy message, half-asleep and secret
In the first flower of dawn.
May He who is the source of all joy
Kiss me likewise into new life
At the end of the old.
May all the dreams of the night flower into new songs
At the moment of awakening.
May she, the Lonely One, who dwells in my heart,
Appear in bridal raiment on the morn of
My new life.

3

The 'I' that floats along the wave of time,
From a distance I watch him.
With the dust and the water,
With the fruit and the flower,
With the All he is rushing forward.
He is always on the surface,
Tossed by the waves and dancing to the rhythm
Of joy and suffering.
The least loss makes him suffer,
The least wound hurts him –
Him I see from afar.
That 'I' is not my real self;
I am still within myself,
I do not float in the stream of death.
I am free, I am desireless,
I am peace, I am illumined –
Him I see from afar.

4

Beyond the shores of Life and Death,
Oh Friend, you are waiting for me.
In the silent sky of my heart,
Your throne is flooded with Light –
With what hope and joy I turn
With outstretched hands towards it.
The silent night has spread its dark tresses
Round your feet.
Tonight, what song filling the whole Universe
Descends to earth from your *vina*!
The earth melts in a flood of melody,
And I lose myself in songs
That breathe sadness.

5

The day is done.
Take away from mine eyes
The veil of light of the setting sun.
In the heart of Darkness lie the springs
Of eternal Light –
Throw them open unto me.
At the end of all words,
Let them merge and become One.
Within the heart of the silent Voice,
Plays eternal the melody –
Whisper into mine ears that melody.

6

When we parted, I thought
Tears would never cease flowing.
Day by day in the dust of the wayside
The flowers wither and drop from my garland,
And I know not
When the veil of forgetfulness came over me.
Slowly my heart had hardened –
I thought tears would never flow again.
Alas, when I met him suddenly at the corner of the road,
Ceaseless tears began to flow.
Behind my forgetfulness
Had tossed eternally the waves of tears.

7

Before the night passes away,
Light the lamp of my life
With your flame, O Beloved.
I am waiting for the evening
When you will come along the path carrying your flame,
And my heart with its brooding darkness
Will light up in a blaze.

8

Water that is imprisoned in the heart of the earth,
The earth finds her not.
When she escapes from her into the distant sky,
And dark clouds draw weird patterns high above,
The earth finds her not.
Then thunder strikes her with the fire of pain,
And the storm drives her wailing in all directions.
The treasure that was once so near
Comes back to the heart again;
In tears she comes pouring down,
And the earth finds her at last.

9

The light has gone out in the dark night,
Come to me with gentle steps.
When you pass this way,
You will know my cottage from the scent of the *champak*
Blossoming by the temple side.
I lie awake all night, and sing in the hope
My songs may reach you.
I fear lest sleep overtake me at the end of the night
And the melodies die out in my tired voice.

10

Oh, wash my soul clean, in the waterfall of this morning light,
Wash away the dust that covers and hides me.
She who is slumbering within me, entangled in the net of sleep,
Touch her forehead gently with the golden rod of early dawn.
The wind that blows from the heart of the Universe,
The life-mad, song-laden wind —
Let my heart bow to her gentle touch.

11

The lamp of earth burns in the lap of Mother Earth.
The evening star looks down wistfully to watch her light;
That light is like the anxious look of the beloved, lost to itself —
It flickers like a fear that throbs within a mother's heart.
That light burns within the heart of the green earth,
And trembles with pain in the restless wind.
The voice of the evening star descends from the heavens,
Bringing benediction,
And the immortal flame is athirst to burn up
In a mortal flame.

12

In the heart of thunder plays the melody —
To its rhythm I awake!
I get drunk with that life
Hidden in the core of death,
To the sound of the tempest's roar
My heart dances in joy.
Tear me away from the lap of ease,
Plunge me into the depths
Where majestic Peace reigns,
In the midst of restlessness.

13

My life's cup is overflowing with the nectar that you filled –
You know it not, you know it not!
Unseen like the flower that fills the night with perfume,
You have filled my heart with your songs –
You know it not, you know it not.
Time has come for parting –
Raise your gracious face and look at me;
With sweet dying I will offer my life at your feet,
She, whom you have not known, not known –
May her silent night of hidden pain end tonight.

14

With the light of mine eyes
I saw the outside;
Now when the light is gone, I see the self within.
In the playhouse of the world I had played with thee –
Let that play be over and the meeting of hearts begin,
The string of the *vina* has snapped,
The *vina* of the heart now sings.

15

Touch me with thy fire,
Burn and purify my life.
Lift my body
And make it thy temple lamp.
Let my songs be the oil
That feeds the flame.
In the core of Darkness
Stars blossom forth at thy touch,
And my agony aflame
Rises to heaven.

Poems of Wonder

To Edith

whose love has sustained me through life
AURO

1   *The Day's End*

When the flute becomes silent
And the light goes out,
When the curtain comes down over life's play,
May there be no gathering of men
To mourn the poet.
May the chairman remain at home playing cards
And not call his memorial meeting!

I know the flowers will remember me.
Wherever the flutes played round me
Celebrating the season's festivals –
In spring, autumn and the rains –
There my seat will be decorated lovingly
In cool, refreshing green,
And my silence filled with the song of birds.

I know this message will echo through the forests:
'To their melodies I strung together the poet's words.'
It will resound in the patter of rain,
In the thunder of clouds,
In the hues of early dawn.

Let my remembrance be cherished
Where the leaves make their rustle
And dews sparkle in fleeting laughter;
Where the shadows sleep in sunlight
And work appears in the guise of play;
Where lighting the lamp in solitude,
Leisure fills the tray of offering
With many-coloured dreams!

25th Vaisakh 1333 (Bengali era), the poet's birthday.

Ask me not,
What is salvation
Or where to find it,
I am not a seeker, but only a poet –
I live close to this earth.
Before me flows the river of life –
Bearing on her stream
Light and shadow, good and evil,
Gain and loss, tears and laughter,
Things that melt away
And are forgotten!
On her waters
The dawn comes with deepening hues,
The sunset spreads her crimson veil,
And moonbeams fall like mother's gentle touch.
In the dark night
The stars chant their prayers;
On her waves
The *madhuri* float their offering,
And the birds pour out their songs.
When to the rhythm of the waves
My heart dances in song,
Then in that rhythm
Is both my bondage and my freedom.
I desire to keep nothing
And cling to nothing.
Untying the knots of union and parting,
I want to float with the All,
Raising my sails to the fleeting wind.

O great Wayfarer,
For you the ten ways* lie open

To the ends of the earth,
You have no temple, no heaven,
No final end.
With every step you touch holy ground.
Walking with you, O restless One,
I find salvation
In the treasure of the journey.
In light and darkness,
In ever-new pages of creation,
In each new moment of dissolution
Echoes the rhythm of your dance and song.

---

* The great circle of the horizon is divided into ten arcs.

3   '*I*' *(1)*

In my consciousness
Emerald is coloured green, ruby red.
I opened my eyes to the sky
And light was kindled in East and West.
I turned to the rose and said: 'Beautiful!'
And it was beautiful.
You will say:
'This is philosophy and not the poet's voice.'
I reply:
'It is truth, therefore poetry.'
This is my pride on behalf of all men:
It is on the canvas of Man's pride,
That the great Artist's art is shown.
The sage mutters counting his beads:
'No, no, no!
No emerald, no ruby, no light, no rose,
No I, no you.'

On the other hand, He who is infinite
Has meditated from within the limits of Man –
It is this which is called 'I'.
In the cave of this 'I' light and darkness were united.
Form appeared, *Rasa* woke.
Then, I know not when, by the incantion of *Maya*,
'No' in lines, in colours,
In joy, in pain,
Bloomed into 'yea'.
Do not call this philosophy;
In the workshop of this universal 'I',
With brush in hand, colour on palette,
I found joy.

The learned have said;
'The old moon with cruel and cunning smile,
Like the messenger of death is creeping towards the earth —
One day seas and mountains will feel her last giant pull.
On earth, in great Time's book,
The new page will be filled with a huge zero,
Devouring all loss and gain;
The deeds of man will lose all claim to eternity
And the ink of endless night obliterate history.
The eye of Man, departing,
Shall wipe the universe's colours all away;
The mind of Man, departing,
Shall wither all *Rasa* dry.
The shadow of violence will shake the heavens,
No light shall burn any more,
The players fingers will play
But no melody arise.'
That day, the Creator bereft of his poetry
Will sit, plunged in thought
Alone in the blueless sky of impersonal existence.
In this endless Universe,
In world after world,
Will nowhere then echo these words:
'You are beautiful,'
'I love'?
Will the Maker sink again in endless meditation,
And counting his holy beads,
Mutter the invocation:
'Speak, O speak!'
'Say, "You are beautiful," '
'Say, "I love." '?

Give me strength, give me courage,
O thou eternally Beautiful!
Give me the sky of contentment,
Give me unending freedom
From the daily trampling of feet in the dust.
Let me not sway
In the boisterous current of the moment,
In the bewildering distraction of grief!
Unwearied courage is in the heart of the *juthi*,
Lovely and gracious;
Though the darts of torrential rain strike it,
It fills its fleeting life with the tune of eternity,
And droops with simple grace on a bed of thorns –
Perfection mirrored in its gentle heart!
Give me that calm courage,
That strength of self-forgetfulness,
Beautiful in its limitation.
Simplicity that knows no doubts –
May it join in a rhythm of peace
All my thoughts, all my utterance.

5 *Deliverance (2)*

To escape far, far from self
I seek your grace, your call,
O Beautiful One, the Invisible:
May the heart-filling melodies of rainy July
Play on my flute,
And make me forget
The restless clamour of my heated surroundings,
The pull of the earth under my feet:
Motionless I wait, all day long, by the wayside.
The day ends, the shadows deepen,
And the tired sun seeks peace beyond the horizon.
As the day strides along without fear
Towards the endless Unknown –
A pilgrim of the trackless, companionless, dark way,
Lost in a song of the Infinite –
So in self-offering bring me out into the open.
Let the void be filled with melodies,
And lead me from path to path,
O Beautiful One, the Invisible!

'O flute-player,
Play your flute,
Let me hear my new name' –
So I wrote you my first letter,
Do you remember?
I am your girl of Bengal;
The Creator did not take full time
To make a human being out of me –
Left me but half-complete.
Between the outside and the inside,
There is not full harmony,
Nor between the past and the present,
Intellect and feeling,
Desire and ability;
He did not put me in the ferry-boat of Modern Age,
But stopped me on the yonder bank
Of the stream of Time.
There in the sharp light
I dimly see the distant world,
My poverty-stricken world for no reason
Becomes restless,
Stretches out both hands
But cannot reach a thing.
The day will not end;
I, looking at the flood, wait –
See the ferry-boat
To yonder shore of freedom float away;
Just then your flute plays
With the melody of full life,
And in the dead vein's pulsing
The stream of Life recurs.
What tune do you play?
Who knows what anguish it raises

In the heart of someone?
You play perhaps
The songs of southern winds
And the song of new youth.
I hear it, I feel it —
The trickling mountain stream has swollen,
And resounds with the thunder of monsoon.
At early dawn, rising, I see
The banks are washed away,
And the restless whirl of current
Tosses the stubborn stones.
In my blood your melody brings
The call of the storm,
Of the flood, of the fire,
Brings the death-dealing call of the Ocean,
The chain-shaking call of the wild wind!
In the narrow creek of the Incomplete
Comes snatching away, floating away,
The full stream's rushing plunder!
The scourging of the rain-laden April storms,
Like the forest's fury
Whirls round the body.

God has not given me wings —
Only your songs have touched my dreams
With the rainstorm's madness.

At home I work meekly,
Everyone says: 'Good'.
They find there is no strength in my desires,
Nor greedy hankering;
With the slightest gust of wind
I'm thrown into the dust.
I am not brave enough
To push the prohibiting guard away.
I do not know how to love severely,

I know only how to weep.
O, flute-player:
When I hear you play,
The call comes to me from the world of Immortals –
There, I raise my head in glory,
There, my life is like the youthful sun
Unclouded by the veil of mist,
There, my zeal heeding no prohibition
Spreads its wings of fire,
And like the hungry bird of God*
Flies to the unknown void.
The rebel in me awakes,
And with a scornful look
Condemns the coward crowd around.
O, flute-player!
Perhaps you wanted to see me;
I do not know, for our meeting
Which is the right place
Or the right time,
Nor how you should recognize me.
In the lonely rainy night,
Ringing with the cricket's chirp,
She, shadow-like, has gone
To meet you.

Hearing your call,
The tame, lifeless girl
Came out of the dark corner –
A woman unveiled!
She is like the first verse
That suddenly poured from *Valmiki*'s† heart,
And enthralled you!
She will not come down from her seat of Song.
She, sitting under the shadow of melodies,
Will write your letters –
Where she lives, you will never know.

O, flute-player,
Let her remain in the far-distance
Of your flute's melody.

16 June 1936

---

† The author of the Ramayana, *Valmiki,* is supposed to be the first poet
of the human race. He was originally the chief of a robber band, which
performed human sacrifices to the goddess. The story tells how, seeing the
appealing look of a young girl brought for sacrifice, his heart melted and
a line of verse (in Sanskrit) poured out of his heart spontaneously – the first
line of verse that ever issued out of a human voice. Tagore, when only 21,
immortalized the story in an opera, *Valmikipratibha.*

*Jarati**

O *Jarati*,
I have seen your picture in my heart.
At the end of night,
The steady flame of the lamp
Bathes your brows, lips, white hair.
The serene light of the morning star,
Like a benediction,
Falls upon your steady eyes.
At twilight,
The dying perfume of the garland
Has made the air sad,
And fades out like the last notes of the *vina*
At the end of a festival.
The moist, dew-drenched air stirs slowly
And the branches of the *asath* are motionless.
The slender, clear stream of the river
Noiselessly flows towards its deserted home,
Like the tired steps of the beloved left behind.
O white-haired *Jarati*,
I have seen you in life's autumn sky,
In the rainless, pure, white clouds.
Below lie the fields filled with corn
And the river is full to the brim.
In the stillness of perfection
The earth is profound in its loveliness.
O *Jarati*,
I have seen you on the last shore of Being,
When the din of Time is drowned
In the fathomless depths.
In the night,
After your pilgrim's bath in the waveless sea,
With unbound hair you bow before the altar,
And worship the Perfect End.

From the heart of the Restless
Where dwells eternal peace,
On your gentle head pours grace extreme,
Like the last rays of the sun
Setting behind the unplumbed waters
Of *Manoswara.*†

---

* A very old woman.
† A sacred lake in Western Tibet, to which thousands of Hindus go on pilgrimage every summer. It also means the lake of the Mind.

8

Woman

Nectar and Joy taking form in Woman,
Have lifted restless waves to subdue
The male, proud in his isolation.
Behind the mystery of God's *Tapasya*
The sculptor seeks the pristine form in thought,
And has tried to capture in his own creation
This ephemeral beauty.
He has cast aside fear and shame,
The injunctions of the scriptures,
And made the Nude pure
Beyond the reaches of sensual pleasure.
The infinite pain in the heart of man
Thirsting for divine nectar in the earth's wine,
Scatters its trail
In song, canvas and stone.
Age after age, country after country,
Untouched by langour,
Unsoiled by weakness,
One beholds her beauty
In the dream of the artist.
The mind of Man – banished from heaven –
Draws to itself the Splendour of the Universe
And effects the union of Form with the Formless!

9

Your salutation is like a jewel
That adorns her you welcome.
The pure stainless light in which your eyes,
Lit with adoration, see her,
Has bathed her entire being
And touched her brow with the mark of greatness.
Be she a goddess, or only woman,
The rays scattered from your heart
Surround her with divine light;
Her true face has found in you
Its voice of victory,
And your love has brought forth
The radiant grace of her being.
The nectar that she drinks,
Pours out from your overflowing heart.
Even as the splendour of dawn crowns the rising sun,
So shall God's revelation crown your head
As it touches the earth in bowed reverence.

10   *The Dying Year**

The journey ends,
The shadows of death thicken
At the end of the western path.
The setting sun, prodigal at parting,
With both hands scatters its treasures.
In the riot of colours, I see
The luminous horizon of death,
The grandeur of life.

My breath will cease,
With these my parting words:
'How much I have loved!'
The eternal mystery, overflowing its banks,
Has made into one, life and death,
And filled day and night
My cup of pain with nectar.

Alone I have travelled
The hard pilgrim's path of Sorrow,
Beaten by the scorching sun of April!
How many a day
Have I been companionless,
How many a night
Without a lamp!
And yet within my heart
I have felt his touch.
Calumny's garland of thorn
Again and again has pierced me –
This I have taken as my bridal wreath.

Gazing on the illumined face of the earth
With steady eyes,

---

* The Bengali New Year is in the month of April, the hottest time of
the year.

Wonder without end has filled me.
Lakshmi, who dwells among a thousand lotuses,
Has touched all my body and soul;
The breath of the world's tears and smiles
I have imprisoned in my flute.

Those who, incarnate as Man,
Have uttered the Word –
Divine and inexpressible –
They are my kin.
How many a time have I lain defeated
In fear and shame!
And yet in my voice has echoed
The victory of the Infinite.
Though my worship is imperfect,
Yet from time to time my weeping soul
Has flung open the prison-gates.

In this life I have received
The birth-right of Man –
This is my good fortune.
For me is the divine nectar,
That flows through the Ages
In thought, knowledge and work.
The perfection,
Whose image glows bright in my heart,
I know is for all to share.

Sitting in meditation on my carpet of dust,
I have seen the Supreme Being,
Bathed in the Light that is beyond all light.
Less than the smallest grain,
Greater than all greatness,
Is He –
Him I have found beyond the reaches of sense.
Piercing the veil of my body,

I have seen in sudden flashes
The unquenchable flame.

Wherever a man of God
Has made a burnt offering,
In its blessing I have my share;
Whenever a man has freed himself
From the shackles of illusion,
In him I know myself;
Whenever the fearless hero has conquered death,
In that history I hold my place.

He who is excellent beyond all excellence,
To him I bow down,
Though often I forget to chant His name.
The blessings of the silent heavens,
The ecstasy of early dawn,
Have touched my heart.
In this world full of wonder,
In this life full of grandeur,
Death shall bring me completion.

Today, this last day of the year,
When the time for parting has come,
O Death, remove thy veil!
So many things have dropped away,
I know, I know —
So much affection, so many loves!
The lamp has died out
Leaving no remembrance.
Thy hand, O Death, is full
With the moment that is deathless;
And thine, O End,
With the treasure that is endless.

30th Chaitra, 1333 (last day of the Bengali year)

11   '*I*' (2)

I wonder if I know him
In whose speech is my voice,
In whose movement is my being,
Whose skill is in my lines,
Whose melody is in my songs
In joy and in sorrow.
I thought he was chained within me,
Contained by tears and laughter,
Work and play.
I thought he was my very self
Coming to an end with my death.

Why then in a flood of joy do I feel him
In the sight and touch of my beloved?
This 'I' beyond self I found
On the shores of the shining sea.
Therefore I know
This 'I' is not imprisoned within my bounds.
Losing myself, I find him
Beyond the borders of time and space.
Through the Ages
I come to know his Shining Self*
In the life of the seeker,
In the voice of the poet.

From the dark clouds pour the rains.
I sit and think:
Bearing so many forms, so many names,
I come down, crossing the threshold
Of countless births and deaths.
The Supreme undivided, complete in himself,

---

* In the *Upanishads* God is evoked as the 'Shining Self'.

Embracing past and present,
Dwells in Man.
Within Him I shall find myself –
The 'I' that reaches everywhere.

21 February 1931

12 *A Picture*

I have drawn you line by line with my brush.
From the depths of the voiceless
I have brought you into this world,
Where praise and blame are apportioned.
For this arrogance of mine
Are you nursing your complaint
Against your maker?
So long as you remained unmanifested,
The world's myriad forms clamorously danced
To the rhythm of creation and destruction.
You waited in the void
For an artist to hear your silent cry,
And hold you fast
Within the limits of light and shadow,
Black and white.
I was passing by the way,
When your appeal pierced the empty space of non-being
And touched my forehead silently –
As a dream half-articulate.
From the sea of the formless
I have brought you into the world of lines;
Is that pain reverberating somewhere
In the heart of form?
Because of a flaw in beauty,
Must my work stand ashamed,
Not honouring enough the truth of existence?
Be it so –
For a deadly error in form does not remain forever,
But dies of its own heaviness.
And you will be free again,
Merging into the sea of the formless, the inexpressible!

13 *Judgement*

Do not judge —
Where you live is but a small corner of this earth.
So far as your eyes reach,
They encompass so little,
To the little you hear,
You add your own voice.
You keep good and bad, black and white,
Carefully apart.
In vain you make a line
To draw a limit.

If a melody is hidden within you,
Awaken it as you go along the road.
In song there is no argument,
No call to work —
He who pleases will respond,
He who pleases not will pass it by.
What matter if some men are good
And some are not?
They are all travellers of the same road.

Do not judge.
Alas, time flies by
And all debate is vain.
Look, the flowers blooming at the forest's edge,
Bring a message from the sky,
For she is a friend of the earth;
In July rains
The grass floods the earth with green,
And fills her cup to the brim.
Forgetting self,
Fill your heart with simple joy.
Traveller,
Scatter freely along the road
The treasure you gather as you go.

14 *The Unknown*

In the crowded market-place I see a thousand faces –
A thousand histories come and go
In the light of the day,
In the shadow of the night.
Through all future time
None will ever know their full story.

Deep down beneath their loud disputes,
Their ceaseless babble,
Goes on the vast and varied work of creation –
Half-remembered and half-forgotten.

No sound nor light is there:
From the untold past, these hidden voices,
These unheard histories of countless men,
Flow like subterranean streams
To the ocean of death.
What has become of them?
What is their purpose?

O beloved,
Hearing you, seeing you, and touching you –
What little I know of you is nought
Compared to the vast, unseen, unheard mystery
That lies locked up – awaiting whom?
The key to that chamber is not with you –
In whose hands is it then?
The Great Unknown,
Does He know the unknown hidden in our hearts
And is all other love surpassed by His –
Before whose benign gaze
What was obscure raises its veil?

I shall not blame you.
All the wounds and failings of our life
That are hurting you,
Come from the frown of fate.
I know you are not away
In the far distant heaven,
But dwell in me
And carry all my burden night and day.
Surmounting our impassable barrier,
Let there be unceasing flow of give and take.
May I strive
By my own effort, to lighten this burden,
To untie the tangled knots of bondage,
And forgetting self, walk the wide world
Without strife, without constraint.
Banishing all unrest,
You and I together will make a melody,
That rises up to heaven.

I came from far away down the stream of Time.
When I arrived on the shores of your Age,
I had no companions,
For they landed at a different harbour.
The little-known joys, the gifts of my heart,
I have given away utterly
Coming down the stream.
In my time,
When I put my feet upon this life,
My claims upon it grew step by step –
Through work and thought,
Language and gesture,
The give-and-take of daily life.
In laughter and play,
Somehow to carry on by mere presence,
Somehow to crowd the stage of life –
That was enough.
Today in your Age I am a stranger.
Our language has taken a new meaning on your lips,
The seasons have changed,
Even the winds are topsy-turvy,
Little differences rise up
And jostle in laughter.
Tastes, hopes, desires
Which make up the colour of life –
All have changed.

The companionship that I gave in my time,
However little may have been its value,
Still it binds together man to man
And gave the Age its character;
That companionship of mine cannot be measured
By the foot-rule of your time.
The flowers that decorate the banquet of these days,

Do not grow in my garden.
I cannot pay rent for the corner I occupy
In your mansion.
Therefore I have to give greatly in utter daring —
This gift is not to satisfy the demands of the Present.
Therefore if it is not to your liking,
Its appraisal can be left to the Future.
And yet with what I have,
I must not only pay off my debts to the Present,
But hope that this Present may be in my debt.
That which is beyond loss and profit,
That which is greater than mere joy and suffering —
May I offer utterly,
Without weighing the balance sheet
Of praise and blame.

The Pitcher

Lord, who art worthy of worship,
O Lord of my life!
You know my caste is low —
Yet pushing past all other doors
Why did you come to me?
Carrying my pitcher in the scorching midday sun,
I was hastening
Home by the winding path;
From me you asked for water!
I am a low-caste woman,
How dare I pollute you?*
Unloading my pitcher,
I touched your feet with my forehead
And said: 'Do not make me guilty.'
Hearing me, you rested your eyes upon me
And smiling, said:
'O thou, who art moulded of earth —
Even as the globe of earth is holy,
Filled with the loveliness of green,
So art thou the seat of *Lakshmi*.
Beauty has no caste,
She is free.
Rosy dawn decks her in jewels,
And for her the night weaves
His garland of stars.
Hear my words:
The many-petalled lotus,
That grows out of slime,
Has no caste.
Is she impure on whom shines
The pure delight of the heavens?
Where the Lord has joy in his creation,

---

* It was the custom, among high-caste Hindus, not to accept drinking
water from those of low caste. If they did, they felt themselves polluted.

There shower incessantly
The blessings of the universe.'
Uttering these words, water-laden,
With the thunderous voice of a cloud,
You went away.

Since then,
Each day in the light of the dawn
I paint this fragile vessel in many colours,
To cover up its earthiness.
O Excellent One!
May Beauty's sacred offering
Be held towards you
By her whom you accepted,
Descending from your throne.

24 July 1932

By the curtain of this mortal world
My mind is veiled.
She sees me by signs and flashes,
In light and darkness,
Half-guessing, half-proving,
Mixing with all this
Her hopes, her thirst
And her own designs.
Sometimes improving me a little
She sees me afresh;
Often doubts have arisen.
How many a day has passed by
On the shores of this home, our world.
She loved it, she played with it,
But, ending all, has gone.
I wonder:
If in the world beyond
Her heavenly eyes,
Illusion-freed, see me,
Shall I be the same self?
However well she knew me,
Still I remained as unclear to her,
As she to me.
O Man,
Perfect light is but destruction.
The Creator's sleight of hand
Plays hide and seek in light and shadow.
In that *Maya* we had built together our playroom,
And were enthralled by the illusion of the Imperfect.
In the vessel of this earth I tasted divine nectar —
The Perfect is only the cruel,
The Uncovered, the silent.

19 *Birthday**

The sun in its round
Has returned to the day of my birth,
Stringing together the scorching days,
And the beads of my rosary come to their last knot.

O thou, the *Tapswi*,
Open thy hands and accept my garland.
Austere is thy seat of meditation –
There I brought to thee day by day,
In the glare of the midday sun,
In the storm of the monsoon,
My stern hymns of praise.
Leave thy meditation and descend
Where the forests are thick with shadows,
And the dawn tender with the touch of rains;
Where the weary twilight scatters in the skies
Her magic of colours,
And the evening star, voiceless and solitary,
Lights the *Arati*
To dedicate her offering to the Infinite;
Where the green and hospitable earth,
Bathed in peace and loveliness,
Brings to the heart her manifold pleasures
In forms, savours and songs.

On the threshold of this world
Let me take my leave today,
And free myself from the fetters of work.
I shall wander –
Picking flowers scattered by the wanton wind,
Gathering songs that float over birds' nests,
Awakened to life at the touch of light.
This touch of the Universal Being,
This joy of hidden life in earth, sky and water,

In the twilight of my life
I shall lift to the very core of my heart –
Into mine eyes, voice and blood,
Into my sleep, awakening and meditation.
In the dusk of this life,
I shall fill my heart, mind and body,
For the last time,
From the ocean of the universe.
I cast away
All labour, disputations and doubts,
Vain hopes and ambitions,
And shall depart with these my last words:
'I go, I leave my love behind.'

---

* Written on the poet's birthday in May, the hottest time of the year in Bengal.

20

I awake again!
The night has waned
And the universe unfolds its petals –
This is wonder without end!
Continents have submerged,
Stars have extinguished their lights,
And epochs have come to an end.
World-conquering heroes have faded behind legends,
Nations have raised their columns of triumph
In the slime of blood,
To satisfy the insatiable hunger of the dust.
Amid the flood of that great destruction
My forehead receives the consecration
Of the first rays of early dawn,
At the end of another night –
This is wonder without end!
Today,
I stand amidst the assembly of stars –
I am one with the Himalayas,
One with the *Saptarishi.*
I am there, where the waves dance
To the boisterous laughter of *Rudra,* the Terrible!
Centuries, that witnessed the rise and fall of sceptered crowns,
Have left their seal
In the rings of this most ancient tree;
Under her shade I am privileged to sit
For one more day –
This is wonder without end!

21 *The Door*

O Door,
You remain ever open.
But the eyes of the blind are closed –
He knows not what is within,
He fears to enter.

O Door,
Night and day your solemn call is never silent,
You open yourself to the rising sun,
And at night to the stars.

O Door,
From seed to the blossom,
From flower to the fruit,
From one era to another,
From Death to Immortality,
You open the way.

O Door,
Life passes through the gateway of Death.
At your behest, in the night of despair,
Along the path of deliverance
Rings the call 'Fear not.'

22   *Life (1)*

Through aeons and aeons the stars shine;
In the flow of Time, out of fleeting darkness
Swirling flames flare up –
In that stream this earth is but a bubble of dust.

On it, for the briefest moment
The spark of life holds forth its tiny light
Like a temple lamp,
To worship at the feet of the Infinite.

Otherwise the sound of the conch* would not have echoed
In the temple of Eternity,
And the chant of the *Samamantra*
Had remained unsung.

---

* The conch shell is blown to call people to worship.

23

Long ago I offered my heart to thee,
But thy gentle tears anointed it not,
Nor did the dew of tender feelings cool it.
The flowers have faded
And no garland adorns thy neck.
It seemed I saw tenderness
Glistening in thine eyes,
But it vanished with faded flowers.
If, while treading this earth,
A seed had dropped from thy hands —
New life, as immortal fruit
Would have returned to thee.

24

When Spring departs
She leaves with a smile
The touch of flowers
On forest's brow.

Even so, a smile shall bloom,
And with dancing rhythm
A flower drop as you leave.

Your barque shall glide away,
And I, left behind,
Shall gaze afar!

When the setting sun
Pours his golden rays
On your sail,
Blackness reigns
In the heart of night.

25

O Friend! I know you –
But this is not the full truth!
I know the many of everyday life
Who, during work and leisure,
Rise up in clear outlines
Within their limits.
I deal with them in daily life
And receive my due –
Nothing more!

Amid the churning of the Oceans
You rode out of the depths
And entered my life.
From there you bring the dim and the obscure,
That envelops you like nebula
Encircling a star.
The artist has closed you in with his warning fingers:
Only thus far – the rest is silence!
Beauty that guards the inner shrine
Keeps me from you, far away.

26

Wake him not, wake him not!
He owes defeat to cruel Fate,
And longs to drown all desires
In fathomless deep.
May the burden of unbearable sighs vanish
And profound sleep come like black ink,
Blotting out from memory's page
The mocking words of the Past.
Let the murmurs of his anguish be hushed,
And grow silent
Like the quiet nest of sleeping birds.

27   *Coming and Going*

Love comes with silent steps
As in a dream!
As she departed the door creaked –
I rushed out to call her back,
But the dream went bodiless,
Vanishing in the dark.
The flicker of the candle from afar –
A mirage red like blood!

28

Let me hear –
With ears to the ground I lie.
The day wanes,
The birds sing their last, pouring out all
That is still stored in their voices.
They draw me to the life
Where melodies play and colours splash.
Their story carries just this message:
'I exist, I live this very moment' –
It reaches my heart.
My mind,
Like pitchers filled by women at dusk,
Plunges in the sky's immensity,
And fills it with life's song.
Give me leisure
To spread out my mind at the day's ebb.
All around me in fading light –
The silent joy of the trees,
The hidden joy in my marrow,
The scattered joy amongst the leaves!
My mind drinks in life's sap
Filtered through consciousness.
Let me sit and gaze.

You come and argue!
At the day's end, when shadows deepen,
I find my leisure –
It is beyond praise or blame,
Good or bad;
It knows no strife, nor wavering,
But only –
The green of the forest,
Light's play on water,
On life's stream

A little tremor,
A little murmur,
A little wave!
In sunset sky like butterflies
My leisured hours fly past
To end the play of their coloured wings.
Do not argue.
Why bring your many claims?
My back to the Present,
I face the Past.
Once, this life
Pursued by many griefs,
Played out its part,
When light and shadow
Wove a pattern in forest glade.

In autumn's noon
On tremulous grass,
The wind's soliloquy
Played on my flute.
All worry, all care,
That twine round life,
Are swept away.
Hurrying forward, the traveller leaves behind
All effort, anxiety, desire.
This only whispers through the leaves:
'They too have lived.'
I feel today:
The tremor of the coloured veil,
The wind's sigh,
The backward-calling gaze,
The rhythm blossoming into love.

29

Hope

Long have I cherished the hope –
In a corner of this earth to live by myself alone.
Neither riches, nor honour, only a tiny hut –
This I have hoped for.
The cool shade of the tree,
The silent flow of the river,
The evening-star at twilight's end,
The scent of *chameli* by the window,
The first light of dawn at the water's edge –
With all these I shall fill my days
In tears and laughter.
Neither riches, nor honour,
Only a tiny hut –
This I have hoped for.

Long have I cherished the hope –
The meditation of my heart,
Shall find its full voice.
Neither riches, nor honour,
Only my own utterance –
This I have hoped for.
The setting sun paints in the clouds
The picture of fulfilment
Dipped in colours of fancy;
Likewise I shall create my *Maya*,
With shade and light
In the world of dreams.
With all these I will fill my days
In tears and laughter.
Neither riches, nor honour,
Only the blossoming of my thoughts
– The fruits of meditation –
This I have hoped for.

30 *Life (2)*

I do not want to die in this beautiful world,
But live in the hearts of men,
And find a niche in the sun-sprinkled, flowered forest.
The play of life heaves like waves
With its tears and smiles,
Meeting and parting!
Stringing together
Man's joys and sorrows,
I want to build on this earth
My eternal home.
Ever new flower-songs I bring to blossom,
For you to gather them, dawn and dusk.
Take them smiling –
And alas, when they wither
Scatter them far away.

31

Lord, I love
The peace that dwells in the rice-fields
Stretching to the farthest horizon,
The sound that echoes
In the clear light of the Blue,
The charm that plays rippling music
In lonesome river-banks.
My hut is enfolded in winds, sky and light,
In content, joy and happiness.
Yet when thy Messenger comes with the Call,
Give me the strength to throw all away,
And accept joyfully the burthen of thy work
Through death and suffering.

32

Through many years,
At great expense,
Journeying through many countries,
I went to see high mountains,
I went to see oceans.
Only I had not seen
At my very doorstep,
The dew drop glistening
On the ear of the corn.

33

The life that flows through my veins, day and night,
Dances in wondrous rhythm in the heavens.
Courses through the pores of the earth,
Scattering joy to leaves, flowers and grains.
Year after year, life and death swing in step
With the ebb and flow of the oceans.
That life everlasting throbs through my limbs,
Giving them majesty,
And the heart-beat of Ages
Dances in my nerves.

In the silence of the night, with moistened eyes,
You kissed me and whispered:
'If you leave me,
The weight of this unending void
Shall crush me,
And my world turn cruel.
The sky-spread weariness
Shall drive all peace away;
Grief – dark, joyless, voiceless!
Death worse than death!'

Hearing this,
I drew you close to my heart
And whispered:
'If you go away
You will echo in my songs,
And pain, like lightening, flash through them.
Withdrawing, you will find the door to my heart,
And in my world, your home.'

The stars heard our whisperings
And their message wafted through the forest-flowers.
Then, silently came death's parting,
And hushed were our exchanges.
And yet that void is no mere emptiness!
The sky is veiled with anguish-laden mists,
And in the fire of that anguish
I create my songs,
My world of dreams!

Awaiting

In your sleep,
At the threshold of your dreams,
I wait and gaze silently on your face
As the morning star first appears at your window.
In the same way, by the sea-shore,
The ascetic plunged in meditation
Gazes towards the East –
His hours of vigil pass away in sleepless ecstasy,
As he looks forward to his immersion
In the first light of morning.

With mine eyes
I shall drink the first smile
That blooms on your half-open lips
Like a flower-bud –
This is my wish.

36

Oh Sorrow,
When unbearable agony floods the heart,
And the Watchman
Bars all doors to consolation,
Coming from outside –
Then does the mind draw sustenance
From its inner depths,
And drops of nectar flow as tears.
This *Ananda* blossoms in the 'I',
Which makes all sorrow, all suffering
Its very own.
In that profound darkness
I find the quenchless light in my heart,
And comprehend:
Heaven dwells for ever within me.

S. S. Andes, 4 November 1924

37

The End

If in your heart you have found the supreme End,
And in your *vina* all discords
Merge into sweet harmony;
If the settting sun calls you back,
As he leads the day towards the dark Unknown,
And in worship of the Beautiful
Pours out his last rays;
If the evening star under the dome of the Infinite,
Shows how burns the lamp of Peace;
If the night opens her door of Silence,
And leads one gently to the pilgrim-shore
Where all voices merge into the great Ocean;
If you have inhaled the scent of the lotus,*
That floats on the lake of the Mind
As last offering, as last salutation –
Then end the day, and let work rest.

38

Standing on the threshold
Where creation's drama unfolds,
I see in sudden flashes
The realm beyond Darkness,
Where immersed I lay
In consciousness of the Great Being –
Unexpressed is He,
Unperceived, Unknown!
In this dawn
The words of the *Rishis* rise to my mind:

---

* The symbol of purity. The Buddha in meditation is seated on the lotus.

'Oh Sun! remove the veil that covers thy light!
In thy perfect light
May I see my true self.'
The self that at journey's end
Mingles its breath with the air,
And transforms the body to dust —
May he not disguised as Truth
Cast a shadow on life's path!

In the playground of this world,
In joy, in suffering,
I have beheld in sudden flashes
The Infinite behind the veil of the finite;
Have comprehended:
The meaning of this birth lay
In that Beauty ineffable,
In that Song inexpressible!
When the drama ends,
I shall leave behind
In this earth's temple —
My salutation,
My worship,
Whose value death cannot grasp

24 January 1941

39

My life is nourished by the river,
And through its veins
The gifts of many mountain peaks run down;
Its fields grow richer from many rivers' silt!

The wondrous sap of life
Feeds the fields from many sources.
Its dream and its awakening
Are circled by many streams of songs
That flow from East and West.

The river – messenger of the Universe –
That brings near the Far,
And brings, even to one's door,
The welcome of the Unknown,
That river has wound all my birthdays into one!
My nest, moving in its stream,
Freed of fetters
Floats from shore to shore.
Not twice-born am I,
Nor have I received the sacred thread*
I am but a wanderer;
The tray of my birthday is ever renewed
With gifts from everywhere –
Gifts given away without a thought.

23 February 1941

---

* One belonging to a low caste who, unlike the Brahmin boy, has not gone
through the ceremony of investiture with the sacred thread. The Brahmin
is called *dvija!*, the twice-born, because his first birth is the physical birth
from the mother's womb, whereas his second birth is into the spiritual
world when he receives the sacred thread. Tagore, the Brahmin-born,
identifies himself with the lowest of the low.

SOURCES

Poems of Hope and Defiance

Poems of Wonder

4	*Parisesh*	46
5	,,	47
6	*Shyamali*	57
7	*Parisesh*	154
8	*Sanai*	75
9	*Parisesh*	97
10	,,	43
11	,,	31
12	,,	171
13	,,	128
14	,,	135
15	,,	149
16	,,	151
17	,,	166
18	,,	141
19	,,	23
20	,,	133
21	,,	50
22	,,	156
23	*Sanai*	25
24	,,	30
25	,,	20
26	,,	29
27	,,	16
28	*Shyamali*	26
29	*Vichitra* (1961 Anthology)	625
30	,,	456
31	,,	564
32	,,	668
33	,,	562
34	*Purabi*	67
35	*Parisesh*	93
36	*Purabi*	136
37	,,	141

GLOSSARY

Amrita, a divine nectar that makes one immortal

Ananda, the ecstatic joy of the soul

Arati, the waving of a garland of lights before the image of a deity during *puja* (performance of religious rites)

asath, an Indian tree

aswath, the holy peepul tree

Bikhu, the religious mendicant. The Buddhist monk may possess nothing; every morning he goes out with the begging bowl, silently stands before the door of a householder and accepts the alms that are given. Tagore addresses the Buddha as 'The Great Bikhu'.

chameli, an Indian flower

champak,   „   „

Dhyana, meditation

ektara, a one-stringed guitar carried by the *Baul* Singers

Indra, the Lord of Heaven, the presiding deity in the Hindu Pantheon

juthi, an Indian flower

Lakshmi, Goddess of beauty and prosperity

madhuri, an Indian flower

mantra, an incantation, verse or hymn sacred to a deity

Maya, illusion, enchantment, fascination

raga, melody patterns in Indian classical music. A particular *raga* is associated with each time of the day.

Raibahadur, title that used to be given by the British rulers to especially loyal Indians. A *Raibahadur* carried immense power and prestige in the countryside.

Rasa, emotional quality in a work of art

Rishis, the sages of ancient India who composed the *Upanishads*

Rudra, another name for Lord *Shiva*

Rudrani, the terrible one, the aspect of the Goddess in her terrifying wrath

Samamantra, hymn of praise to God contained in the *Sama Veda,* the third of the four *Vedas*

Saptarishi (The Seven Saints), the constellation of Ursa Major

sari, Indian women's dress

sishu, Indian plant

sitar, classical stringed instrument, a simplified version of the *vina*

tambura, tanpura, a sort of lute with three strings and having a gourd for the shell

Tapasya, devotional practices for the attainment of a spiritual or creative goal

Tapswi, Lord *Shiva,* the great ascetic, lost in meditation on the summit of the Himalayas, his eternal abode

tilak, tika, a mark on the forehead made with sandle-paste or vermillion, a sign of victory or blessing

vina, a classical stringed instrument, plucked like the harp

Vajrapani, the Vedic Jupiter, *Indra,* the Wielder of Thunder.

INDEX OF TITLES AND FIRST LINES

DATE DUE